LIVY'S HISTORY OF

ROME

BOOK TWO

TITUS LIVIUS
LUCAS WAGNER

CONTENTS

INTRODUCTION

TITUS LIVIUS' GROUNDBREAKING SERIES *Ab Urbe Condita,* known as the "History of Rome" in the English-speaking world, details the founding of Rome and the establishment of the Roman Republic, covering the years 753 BC through 167 BC.

Livy's life overlapped the lives of Jesus Christ and the Emperor Augustus. Just as descriptions of their works had to be recopied by hand over many generations of humans, so too did Livy's. Most of his work did not survive the journey. Today, of the 142 original books in Ab Urbe Condita, only 35 books have survived. The books that remain contain lessons that have outlasted governments, cultures, and entire civilizations.

The sources Livy used to write his history are largely lost. In fact, for some historical events, Livy represents our only surviving record.

As Livy says in his Preface, he wrote these things down because he believed that human civilization is cyclical, calling these stories "shining memorials" which can be used by people in the future. The political philosopher Niccolò Machiavelli agreed, observing that Livy's first ten books allow us to see the impact of decisions, good and bad, across many generations of human civilization. We see patterns and cycles of power, leadership, and behavior. These broad cycles, when studied, allow us to anticipate the future. As Cicero once said, history *is* the teacher of life.

I find that reading Livy is a journey that changes people, both privately and as a citizen of a republic. A fresh understanding of how incredibly difficult and violent it is to create a stable and capable republic will change you as a leader, whether you lead people today or not. The journey has been called many things. Shocking. Uplifting. Funny. Boring. Exciting. Violent. Relatable. Tedious. Powerful. All these descriptions are true.

This version is the first 21st century translation and it follows the conventions of English as spoken in our time. In quoted dialogue, characters speak as they would speak today. Livy, when compared to the translation of Benjamin Foster over 100 years ago, speaks much more informally. We use common contractions (e.g., "don't") that readers expect. That said, we still skip uncommon or archaic ones (e.g., "'twas"). Ornate and verbose English language habits of the 19th and 20th centuries have been stripped away so that the underlying Latin is clearer.

Above all, this work is designed to be accessible and for people to enjoy. To do this, sometimes we need to add to the work. I have written chapter titles and subtitles for you to enjoy, to jog your memory, and to make it possible to "fall forward" and skip to the next subtitle. In Book I, Livy included so many names and places that, at least in the public domain versions, people can tend to quit reading before the best stories even begin. In this version, I want to help you keep moving so that you can finish the book. Fall forward to the next subtitle, but do not quit.

As Machiavelli says, while many tend to believe their state will live forever, all governments have a shelf life. Tyrants quickly rise from the perpetual fires of ailing republics. Nowhere is this clearer than in the struggles of the early Romans. Livy's story is a very human one, and it is one that continues to present day.

Lucas C. Wagner

1 November 2024

Chapter 1

THE FIRST CONSULS: BRUTUS AND VALERIUS (509 BC)

1. FROM THIS POINT on, I'll describe the history of the Roman people, in both war and peace, who are now free. I'll write about their yearly leaders and the supremacy of their laws, which are stronger than any individual. The now-deposed tyrant King Tarquinius' arrogance made this freedom even more appreciated.

NEVER AGAIN

The previous kings ruled in such a way that each king could rightfully be considered as the founder of the part of the City that he had added for the growing population. There is no doubt that the same Brutus who is now praised for expelling Tarquinius would have harmed the public good if he had taken the kingdom from any of the previous kings too quickly in his desire for freedom. The mob of shepherds and foreigners, the plebeians, were refugees from their own lands. Imagine if they had found freedom (or at least no punishment) under the protection of the sanctuary of Rome and then had started to cause trouble and fight with the City's leaders before everyone had time to grow. Imagine if they had done this before they had time to become attached to their new home through their wives, children, and love for the land itself. The entire state would have been torn to pieces by internal problems. Instead, it was the calm moderation of the kings that nurtured the people and allowed them to become strong enough to enjoy the benefits of freedom.

We can consider this time the birth of freedom because, unlike kings, consuls were elected yearly and their authority lasted for only a year. This allowed freedom to flourish much more than a reduction in the authority of the office, which was still similar to the power of a king.

The first consuls, Brutus and Collatinus, had all their privileges and symbols of power, but care was taken so that people wouldn't be too afraid by both having the *fasces*, the bundle of rods and an axe which symbolized authority, at the same time. Brutus would be the first person to have the fasces, with the agreement of Collatinus. He was as eager to protect this new freedom as he had been to establish it.

First, Brutus made the people, still excited about their freedom, swear an oath that they wouldn't allow anyone to be king in Rome. This was to prevent them from being persuaded by the royal family's incoming pleas and bribes. Next, as Tarquinius' murders had reduced the number of senators, he increased the number of senators to three hundred to strengthen them. Leading men of the equestrian rank were selected for this job. Those who were appointed into the new Senate were called Conscripti. The older senators were called Patres. This worked well to promote harmony inside the state and it also brought both patricians and plebeians together.

AN UNPOPULAR NAME

2. The focus then shifted to religious matters. Since some parts of public worship had been performed by the kings themselves, a "king

of the sacrifices" was elected to ensure no aspect was overlooked. This position was made subordinate to the chief priest, the Pontifex Maximus, adding prestige to the title without infringing on the peoples' newfound freedom, which was their main concern.

However, they may have gone too far in their efforts to protect their liberty, even in minor matters. For instance, the people didn't like the name of one of the consuls. The people were disgusted by the mere name of Lucius Tarquinius Collatinus, even though they knew he had done nothing wrong and was on their side.

The Tarquinii family had a long history of ruling; Priscus was the first, followed by Servius Tullus. Even though there was a gap, Tarquinius Superbus, viewing the kingdom as his family's property, reclaimed it through criminal acts and violence. After Tarquinius Superbus was expelled, the government now had Lucius Tarquinius Collatinus as consul and in a position of authority. The Tarquinii family was seen as not being able to live normal, average lives for very long, so even their name was seen as a threat to liberty.

Such discussions gradually spread throughout the state, stirring up the plebeians' emotions. Once it became clear that the issue wouldn't go away, Brutus called a meeting with the people. He began by reciting the oath, which stated that they wouldn't allow a king or any potential threat to their liberty in Rome. Then, he emphasized the importance of defending their freedom at all costs. Brutus was reluctant to speak about Collatinus out of the regard he had for his colleague. However, he told the people that he understood that they didn't feel completely free because the royal family's name wasn't just inside Rome, it was also still at the highest ranks of Roman leadership. This was seen as a threat to their liberty.

Brutus then turned to address Collatinus, asking him to alleviate the plebeians' likely groundless fear. He publicly acknowledged Collatinus' role in expelling the royal family and asked him to renounce his royal name. In return, the citizens would restore his property and provide additional support, if needed. He then urged Collatinus to leave Rome to eliminate the fear of a return to monarchy.

Initially, Collatinus was taken aback. It was an unexpected request from his colleague and he struggled to respond. However, the state's leading figures surrounded him and urged him to comply. They were unsuccessful in persuading him to step down. However, when Spurius Lucretius, his father-in-law and a respected elder, pleaded and advised him to yield to the state's wishes, Collatinus reluctantly agreed because he knew that even if he didn't resign, he still might face future problems and lose his property anyway. He resigned his consulship, moved his belongings to Lavinium, and left the state.

The Senate passed a decree banning Tarquins. Brutus declared that all members of the Tarquin family were to be banished from Rome. In a meeting in the *Comitia Centuriata*, he conducted an election for a new consul. The Centuries voted in Publius Valerius, also known as Publicola, who had helped him expel the king, as Brutus' new colleague.

Tarquinius' "Property" Stratagem

3. Everyone believed that war with the Tarquins was inevitable as they tried to regain power from afar, but it started slower than everyone anticipated. What wasn't expected was that the Romans' newly won freedom was almost lost by deceit and betrayal. Among the young Romans, there were several from prominent families who had enjoyed unrestrained freedom during the reign of King Tarquinius and the Tarquin family. These young men, who were of the same age and friends with the young Tarquins, were used to living like royalty. They

missed these benefits and, now that everyone had equal rights, they felt oppressed. They argued that a king was a person who could be reasoned with, whether for right or wrong reasons. A king could show favor, kindness, anger, and forgiveness. A king could distinguish between a friend and an enemy. Laws, on the other hand, were inflexible and favored the poor over the rich. They argued that it was dangerous to live in a society where human errors weren't tolerated and everyone had to live by strict rules.

As the young Romans continued to work themselves into a state of unhappiness, ambassadors from the Tarquin family arrived unexpectedly. The Ambassadors asked for the return of Tarquin family property, which had been confiscated, but they didn't mention anything about returning to power. The Senate listened to the ambassadors and took several days to consider the request. They feared that refusing the request might lead to a war, while agreeing to it might provide money and resources to the Tarquins so that they could make a war. While this was happening, the ambassadors were quietly working on other things. While their official purpose for being in Rome was asking for the Tarquins' property, they began working on a way to regain the throne. They started to test the waters with the young Romans by privately discussing the idea of the Tarquins returning to power. For those who were sympathetic to the cause, Tarquinius, himself, wrote a personal letter to them, proposing that the royal family be brought back into the City at night, under the cover of darkness.

4. The task of executing this plan was initially given to the Vitellii brothers and the Aquilii brothers. A sister of the Vitellii brothers was married to Consul Brutus; their sons, Titus and Tiberius, were also roped into the plot by their uncles. Several young nobles were also involved, but their names have been forgotten over time.

Meanwhile, the Senate had decided to return the property. The ambassadors used this as an excuse to prolong their stay in Rome, requesting extra time to arrange for the transportation of the royal family's belongings out of the City. This request was granted by the consuls. With little time to spare, the ambassadors then began making formal plans with the conspirators, asking for letters from them to give to the Tarquins. Without these letters, how could the Tarquins believe the ambassadors' reports on such a huge matter? The letters, meant to prove their honesty, ultimately revealed their plot.

The day before the ambassadors left to return to the Tarquins, they had dinner at the Vitellii's house. The conspirators were discussing their plans privately when a slave named Vindicius overheard them and took notice of what was happening. He waited until the letters were given to the ambassadors, knowing that their discovery would confirm the plot. When he saw that the letters had changed hands, he told the consuls everything. The consuls immediately took off from their homes to arrest the ambassadors and conspirators, effectively stopping the plot before anything took place. They took special care of the letters, to ensure they weren't lost, and immediately imprisoned the traitors. There was some hesitation about dealing with the ambassadors. They were seen as enemies, but ambassadors were protected by international law.

SHARING IN SPOILS OF TYRANTS

5. The issue of what to do with all the possessions of the Tarquin family, which the Senate had previously voted on, thus returned back to the Senate. The senators, now enraged, explicitly prohibited these items from being returned to the Tarquins or from being seized by the public treasury. Instead, they were given to the plebeians to be looted.

This was done so that after sharing in the spoils of the tyrants, the people would abandon any hope of reconciling with the Tarquins. The Tarquins' land, a field located between the City and the Tiber River, was seized, dedicated to Mars, and named the *Campus Martius*. At the time, this field was ready for harvest, however, it was considered inappropriate to use the crops. So, the crops were harvested, and a large amount of people hauled off the grain and straw in baskets, dumping them all into the Tiber. The river was shallow due to the summer heat, and the piles of grain became lodged in the shallows and covered with mud. Over time, with the addition of other debris brought by the river, an island gradually formed. I believe that mounds were added later and human intervention helped to strengthen the surface, making it solid enough to support the temples and porticoes there today.

AS ANY FATHER MIGHT FEEL

After the looting of the tyrants' possessions, the traitors were found guilty and sentenced to death. This punishment was particularly noteworthy because Brutus, who was also the father of two of the traitors, was tasked with carrying out the sentence. The young Romans of high status were tied to a stake, but the consul's sons drew the attention of all the spectators. The spectators felt pity for them not just because of the harsh punishment, but also because of the terrible crime they had committed: they came up with these ideas this year, the very same year that Rome had been freed! They had betrayed their countrymen, the gods, and their father, the first consul and a liberator of Rome — all for a ruthless, arrogant tyrant.

The consuls took their seats, and the *lictors*, the bodyguards, were sent to carry out the punishment. They stripped the traitors naked, beat them with rods, and beheaded them. Throughout this, the mob watched Brutus' face for signs of expression. His demeanor was stern, though occasionally his emotions, as any father might feel, surfaced. After the guilty were executed, a sum of money was awarded from the treasury to the person who discovered the crime. This slave, named Vindicius, was also granted freedom and the rights of citizenship. It's said that he was the first person to be freed by the vindicta, a rod that is tapped on the slave's head when freed, and some believe that the term vindicta is derived from his name. From then on, it became a rule that those who were freed in this way were considered to have the rights of Roman citizens.

DESPERATE APPEALS TO "COUNTRYMEN"

6. A detailed report of what had happened reached Tarquinius. As his hopes of returning as king had been dashed, the former king was now filled with a mix of rage and disappointment. Since deception wasn't working, he decided to resort to an open call for war against his former subjects.

He pleaded with Etruscan cities, asking them not to abandon him. After all, he was a man of their own blood, a man who had recently ruled a great kingdom but was now exiled and impoverished. While other kings had been invited to rule Rome from foreign lands, Tarquinius maintained that he had been born into it and had dutifully expanded Rome's empire until he was ousted by a treacherous plot by those closest to him. The Romans had carved up his kingdom among themselves, he maintained, because not one of them was worthy to rule. They allowed his possessions to be looted by the people so that everyone would be guilty of the crimes against him. Tarquinius wanted his crown and his kingdom back at any cost. Then, he would exact revenge by punishing his ungrateful subjects. If the Etruscans would help him, he proposed, they could also avenge the wrongs done to them in the past, as the Romans had defeated their armies and taken their land from them.

Among the Etruscans, his pleas convinced the people of Veii, whose citizens announced that they were eager to erase their past humiliation and regain what they had lost in war, except now under the leadership of a Roman general. The people of Tarquinii were swayed by his name and their shared heritage. They, too, decided to support him, seeing it as an honor that one of their own should rule Rome. Thus, the armies of these two states joined Tarquinius in his quest to reclaim his kingdom and exact revenge on the Romans.

FLAUNTING OUR INSIGNIAS!

As their combined army entered Roman territories, the Roman consuls marched to meet them. Consul Valerius led the infantry in a phalanx formation, while Consul Brutus rode ahead on his horse to scout the enemy. Similarly, the enemy's cavalry was in front. Tarquinius' son, Arruns Tarquinius, led their cavalry, with the king himself following with the legions. While still at a distance, Arruns distinguished Consul Brutus by his escort of lictors. As they drew nearer, he clearly recognized the consul by his features, and, in a fit of rage, exclaimed, "That is the man who drove us from our country! Look at him proudly parading, flaunting our insignias! Gods, avengers of kings, help me now!"

With these words, he dug spurs into his horse and rode straight at the consul. Brutus saw that he was aiming toward him. It was a point of honor in those days for the leaders to engage in single combat, so he eagerly accepted the challenge. They charged at each other with such fury, neither of them thinking of protecting himself and thinking only to wound the other, that each drove his spear at the same moment through the other's shield, and they fell dying from their horses, with their spears still sticking in them.

The rest of the cavalry began to fight, soon followed by the infantry. The battle was evenly matched, with both sides gaining and losing ground. The Veiians, accustomed to being defeated at the hands of the Romans, were routed and fled. The Tarquinians, the new enemy from Tarquinii, not only held their ground but also forced the Romans to retreat.

7. Though the battle ended this way, Tarquinius and the Etruscan armies were so traumatized by the battle that they decided the war should be abandoned for now. They left to return back home in the darkness of night. There are strange stories associated with this battle. It's said that during the quiet the evening they left, a loud voice came from the Arsian Forest. People believed it was the voice of the god Silvanus, saying that because one more Etruscan had died in the battle than had died on the Roman side, the Romans had won the war. Indeed, the Romans left the battlefield as winners, and the Etruscans as losers.

As soon as daylight came and no enemy was in sight, Consul Valerius gathered the spoils and triumphantly returned to Rome. There, he held a grand funeral for his colleague. The public grief was a great honor to Brutus' death. He was especially mourned by the women for a year, as if he were a parent, because he had so strongly and courageously avenged the violation of Lucretia by Tarquinius' son.

VALERIUS' NEW HOUSE

The surviving consul, Publius Valerius, had always found favor with the plebeians, but as public opinion is very fickle and can change easily, he now faced suspicion from the people. Rumors spread that he wanted to be king because he hadn't chosen a colleague to replace Brutus. He was also building an impregnable citadel in a high and well-defended place on top of Mount Velia to use as his private residence. When these rumors reached Valerius, he was upset and called the people to a meeting.

In front of the people, Valerius stood on the rostrum and lowered the fasces, the symbols of authority. The people were pleased to see this sign of respect, and that he acknowledged their power was greater than his. After the people had quieted down, Valerius praised Brutus' good fortune, saying that he had died a hero, defending the commonwealth, at the height of his glory, before it turned into jealousy. Valerius said that he, himself, having outlived his glory, was now the target of accusations and slander.

"Would there ever be any merit enough to protect me from your suspicions?" he asked the people. "How could I, a strong opponent of kings, be accused of wanting to be king? Will my reputation now depend on where I am, rather than who I am? I promise you that my house won't threaten your freedom. I'll move it down to the base of Mount Velia, on level ground, so that anyone can live above me. Now, anyone you decide loves liberty more than Publius Valerius does may live above me!" Immediately, he ordered all materials to be moved to the foot of Mount Velia, and the house was built at the foot of the mount where the Temple of Vica Pota now stands.

8. Following this, a procession of laws followed that not only absolved Valerius from any suspicion of seeking royal power, but also boosted his public image. As a result, Valerius was given the nickname *Publicola*, meaning "one who courts the people." The laws which

were well-received among the people were ones that allowed people to appeal against the magistrates and ones which threatened the life and property of anyone who attempted to seize power to become king. After Publicola passed these laws as the sole consul, earning all the credit, he organized an assembly to elect a new colleague. Spurius Lucretius was elected as consul, but due to his old age and declining strength, he was unable to fulfill his duties and passed away after a few days. Marcus Horatius Pulvillus was chosen to replace Lucretius. Some old records don't mention Lucretius as a consul and instead list Horatius immediately after Brutus. I suspect that because Lucretius' term as consul was uneventful, it was overlooked.

JEALOUSY AT THE TEMPLE OF JUPITER DEDICATION

The Temple of Jupiter on the Capitoline Hill hadn't yet been dedicated. Consul Valerius and Consul Horatius drew lots to decide who would have the honor of dedicating it. The lot fell to Horatius. Valerius left to fight in the war against the Veiians. Valerius' relatives were more upset than they should have been that the dedication of such a famous temple was given to Consul Horatius. They tried everything to prevent it. When all their attempts had failed, they resorted to wickedness. The relatives told Horatius at the very moment he began the ritual of prayer, just as he grabbed the doorpost, that his son had been killed and that he could not continue because his family was now tainted with an omen of death. Whether he didn't believe them or just had incredible self-control isn't known for sure and is hard to guess. He allowed this message to interrupt him only to order that his son be buried. Steadfastly, he finished the prayer and dedicated the temple.

These were the events that took place in the first year after the kings were expelled.

Chapter 2

Lars Porsena's War (508-506 BC)

9. AFTER THIS, PUBLIUS Valerius was elected consul for the second time, along with Titus Lucretius.

At this point, the Tarquin family had sought refuge with Lars Porsena, the king of Clusium. There, they combined their pleas with advice. Sometimes, they implored him not to let them, who were of Etruscan descent and shared the same blood and name, live in exile and poverty. At other times, they suggested that he shouldn't allow the new trend of expelling kings to go unpunished. The allure of freedom is strong. Unless rulers defend their positions as fiercely as the people fight for their freedom, everyone will become equal, the Tarquins argued. There will be no one superior or distinguished, leading to the end of monarchy, the most beautiful form of government among both gods and men.

NOT ONLY THE ENEMY TO FEAR

Lars Porsena believed it would honor the Etruscans to have an ally king in Rome, especially one of Etruscan descent, so he immediately began leading an army towards Rome. In response, the Senate filled with panic unlike anything they had experienced so far. Lars Porsena was famous and Clusium was known to be powerful. They worried not only about their enemies but also about their own citizens. The plebeians, in their fear, might welcome the Tarquin family back into the City, accepting peace even if it meant also accepting slavery.

So, the Senate made many concessions to the plebeians to gain their trust. They focused on the markets, sending people to the Volscians and Cumae to buy grain. The government took over the sale of salt, which had been an overpriced monopoly, and removed it from private hands. The plebeians were also relieved of port duties and taxes, with the burden falling on the rich. The poor were considered to have paid enough if they were raising their children. This considerate approach by the Senate maintained unity during the subsequent hardships of the siege and famine. The dislike for the idea of a king was shared by all, from the highest to the lowest. No single person was as popular as the entire Senate, which was due to their smart governance.

SUBLICIAN BRIDGE: FIRE, SWORD, OR WHATEVER MEANS

10. On the appearance of the enemy, the plebeians in the country fled into the City as best they could. The weak places in the defenses were occupied by military posts. Beyond this, the walls of the City and the Tiber River were deemed sufficient for protection.

However, the Sublician bridge, spanning the Tiber, was a weakness. The enemy would have forced their way over the had it not been for one man, Horatius Cocles. He was the guard at the bridge that day. When he saw the Janiculum Hill taken by surprise attack and the enemy rushing down from there, he noticed his own men were panicking and deserting their posts. He stopped them one by one, appealing to remember their duty to their gods and their people. Running away from the situation wouldn't help, he said. The enemy would easily cross the bridge and soon be on the Palatine Hill and the Capitoline

Hill. In fact, there would be more enemies there than would be on the Janiculum Hill. He shouted at them to, instead, destroy the bridge by fire, by sword, or by whatever means they could, and promised to hold off the enemy as much as one man could.

Cocles ran to the entrance of the bridge, standing out among those who were retreating, and faced the enemy, impressing them with such bravado. Two men, Spurius Larrius and Titus Herminius, also stayed with him due to their sense of honor. The men faced the initial danger and the worst part of the battle together. When those who were tasked with destroying the bridge called for them all to retreat, Cocles made them also move to a safe part of the bridge. He then looked at all the Etruscan officers, challenging them and accusing them of being slaves to tyrants who were trying to take away the freedom of others.

The Etruscans hesitated, looking at each other, unsure of who should start the fight. Eventually, they were moved by shame and started hurling javelins at him from all sides. Cocles held his ground with his shield up, maintaining his position on the bridge. The Etruscans then tried to push him off the bridge, but then retreated in panic when they were interrupted by the sound of the bridge starting to come apart and fall, along with the cheering of the Romans. Cocles then shouted a prayer, "Father Tiber, I solemnly invoke you! Receive these arms and this soldier into your merciful stream!" He then jumped into the Tiber River in full armor, swimming across the river back to the Romans under a shower of Etruscan missiles.

As far as posterity is concerned, in my opinion, Cocles' brave act was likely to be more famous than believable. The City was grateful for his bravery and erected a statue of him in the comitium, the original public meeting space. He was also given as much land as he could plow in one day. The people also showed their appreciation by each giving him something from their own supplies, even though supplies were scarce.

FROM ASSAULT TO BLOCKADE TO TRAP

11. As King Porsena's initial blitz was unsuccessful, he shifted his strategy from assault to blockade. After establishing a military base on the Janiculum Hill, he set up his camp on the plains and along the Tiber River. He then called for boats from all areas to patrol the river, preventing any food or supplies from reaching Rome. The boats were also used to transport his soldiers across the river to raid various locations as needed. In a short time, Porsena made the areas surrounding Rome so dangerous that all resources, including livestock, were moved into the City for protection. No one dared to leave the City gates.

The Romans allowed the Etruscans to move around freely on orders of Valerius. He was waiting for the right moment to surprise a large number of men and chose to hold back his retaliation for a bigger impact. To set a trap for the raiders, Valerius instructed his men to drive their livestock out of the Esquiline Gate, the one farthest from the enemy. He assumed they would learn of this because some slaves would likely betray them due to the blockade and famine. As expected, a deserter informed the Etruscans, and larger than usual groups of the enemy crossed the river in hopes of capturing all the livestock.

Valerius ordered Titus Herminius to hide and lie in ambush with a small group of soldiers two miles from the City on the Gabian Road. He also instructed Spurius Lartius to position himself at the Colline Gate with a group of lightly armed soldiers. They were to block the enemy's return path to the river once they had passed. The other consul, Titus Lucretius, left the City through the Naevian Gate with several maniples of soldiers. Valerius himself led a select group of cohorts down from the Caelian Hill. They were the first to attract attention from the enemy.

Just as planned, when Herminius became aware that fighting had begun, he emerged from his hiding place and attacked the Etruscans who were engaged with Valerius from the rear. Then, soldiers came from both right and left sides, from the Colline and Naevian Gates. The Etruscans were trapped. Not strong enough to fight, yet also not able to escape as all routes had been blocked by the Romans, they were cut to pieces. This put an end to such irregular and scattered raids by the Etruscans.

A SURPRISE ON PAY DAY

12. The siege continued, however. With the protracted blockade came a shortage of grain, which then led to skyrocketing prices. King Porsena still remained hopeful and believed that by maintaining his position, he would eventually wear down and conquer the City.

Caius Mucius, a young Roman nobleman, felt it was a disgrace that the Romans, who had never been confined within their walls during any war nor by any enemy when they were under the rule of kings, were now trapped by the very same Etruscans that they had once conquered. This humiliation, he believed, needed to be avenged by something bold and daring. Initially, he had planned to infiltrate the enemy's camp entirely by himself. However, he feared that if he did so without the consuls' permission or anyone's knowledge, he might be captured by Roman guards and accused of desertion. Given the City's current situation, such a charge would be plausible. So, he decided to approach the Senate. "Fathers," he addressed them, "I plan to cross the Tiber and enter the enemy's camp, if possible. I don't intend to loot. Nor do I seek revenge for their destruction. I have a greater plan in mind, provided the gods are on my side." The Senate gave their approval.

Mucius left, armed with a hidden sword under his robe. Upon reaching the enemy camp, he positioned himself in a densely crowded, near the king's tribunal. Today happened to be the soldiers' pay day. As the soldiers received their pay, Mucius observed that two men seemed to be in charge of the event. They both sat next to each other and wore similar clothing. One of these men was Lars Porsena, he thought, but who was the other man? Soldiers kept coming up to the other man more frequently. Was he Lars Porsena? Afraid to ask, as this ignorance about who was king would betray him, Mucius decided to strike the man who had the respect of the soldiers. Unfortunately, the man he killed was the king's secretary, not the king.

As he tried to flee, pushing through the crowd with his blood-stained dagger, the shouting crowds made it clear where he was. He was immediately seized by bodyguards and brought before King Porsena. Even in this dire situation, Mucius remained fearless, declaring, "I am a citizen of Rome. My name is Caius Mucius. As an enemy I wished to kill an enemy, and I have as much courage to meet death as I had to inflict it. It's the Roman nature to act bravely and to suffer bravely. I'm not alone in having made this resolve against you. Behind me, there is a long list of others who aspire to the same distinction. If it's your wish to continue this war, be prepared for a struggle in which you'll have to fight for your life every hour. A war that will be sending more assassins like me to the very entrance of your royal tent. This is the kind of war which we, the youth of Rome, declare against you. Don't fear an army or formal battles. The matter will be settled between you, alone, and each one of us, individually."

Porsena, both enraged and terrified, demanded to know the details of the assassination plot that Mucius had hinted at. When Mucius didn't comply, the king tried to intimidate him with being burned alive. "Look," Mucius responded, "This is how lightly we regard our bodies when greater glory is in our future." He thrusted his right hand into a fire burning on the altar and showed no signs of pain. The king, shocked by this performance, jumped from his seat and ordered Mucius to be removed from the altar. He told Mucius, "Leave our camp. You have acted more like an enemy to yourself than to me. If you were on my side, I'd praise your courage. Instead, I release you now, unharmed and untouched, exempt from the rules of war."

In response to the king's benevolence, Mucius revealed, "Since you honor bravery, I'll tell you something. Three hundred of us, the best of the Roman youth, have conspired to attack you in this manner. I was chosen by lot to go first. The rest will follow, each in his turn, until Fortune gives us the opportunity to strike you down."

PORSENA SUES FOR PEACE

13. When Mucius was released and returned to Rome, he became known as Scaevola, "the left-handed one," due to the loss of his right hand from the fire. Shortly thereafter, ambassadors from King Porsena followed and came to Rome. The danger of Mucius' initial assassination attempt, which had only been thwarted by an attacker's error, and the repeated risks associated with the numerous conspirators, had gotten to Porsena, deeply affecting him. As a result, he voluntarily proposed peace to the Romans.

Within the peace talks, Porsena talked of restoring the Tarquin family to the throne, knowing it was fruitless and that the Romans would reject it. He did it only because he promised the Tarquin family that he would make this request. Porsena did manage to secure a condition that the Veiians' territory be returned. The Romans were also compelled to release hostages if they wanted Porcena's troops to be removed from the Janiculum Hill and taken out of Roman territory. Once peace was agreed upon, Porsena withdrew his troops from the Janiculum Hill and left Roman lands. In recognition of his bravery, Mucius was awarded lands across the Tiber, which later became known as the Mucian Meadows.

This public honor of courage and valor inspired the women to strive for similar recognition. Near the Tiber, where the Etruscans had set up camp, a young woman named Cloelia, one of the hostages, managed to escape. She led a group of young women hostages across the river, evading enemy attacks, and returned them all safely to their families. When Porsena learned of this, he initially was enraged, demanding the return of the mastermind behind the plot, Cloelia. He didn't care about the other hostage women, just Cloelia. If she wasn't returned, all treaties would be considered invalid.

Porsena soon came to admire her bravery, stating that her actions surpassed those of Cocles and Mucius. He modified his terms, saying that he would still consider the treaties broken if the Romans didn't hand over Cloelia, but that he would give his word that she would return safely and unharmed once she was handed over. Both parties agreed to these terms and the treaties were saved.

The Romans returned Cloelia to King Porsena, who kept his word. Not only did he not harm her, he honored her upon her arrival. After praising her heroism, he offered to release half of the remaining hostages as a gift to her, allowing her to choose who would be freed. She chose the youngest boys, a decision that was both modest and agreed upon by the hostages, themselves, as the youngest were the most vulnerable to abuse.

With peace restored, the Romans honored Cloelia's extraordinary bravery with an equally extraordinary tribute: a statue of her on horseback, placed at the summit of the Via Sacra.

"Goods of King Porsena"

14 The peaceful exit of the Etruscan king from the Janiculum Hill area of the City seems to contradict an old tradition that continues to this day at public auctions. When things that were looted are sold today, it's referred to as "selling the goods of King Porsena." The origin of this practice must have either started during the war and continued into peacetime, or it could have evolved from a more good-natured practice, and not just a notice of the sale of enemy property, as the phrase suggests. The most believable explanation passed down is that Porsena, when leaving the Janiculum Hill, gifted the Romans with his well-supplied camp, which was filled with provisions from the nearby fertile Etruscan fields. The City was depleted from the long siege at the time. To prevent the goods from being mobbed and plundered by the people, they were sold to the people who were allowed in. This was then referred to as the Goods of Porsena. The phrase seems to express more gratitude for the gift than the selling of the king's property, which the Romans never owned.

After ending the war with Rome, Porsena sent his son Aruns and part of his army to besiege Aricia to avoid the appearance of his army having been deployed without achieving anything worthwhile. The Aricians were initially surprised and scared, as they didn't expect this. However, help from the people of Latium and Cumae gave them hope, and they decided to confront the Etruscans in battle. At the start of the battle, the Etruscans' first charge was so fierce that they defeated Aricians immediately. However, the Cumae cleverly moved soldiers to one side. When the Etruscans flew past them in a chaotic charge, the Cumae turned around and attacked them from behind. This stratagem led to the Etruscans, who were close to victory, being surrounded and defeated.

A small group of them, having lost their general and with no other refuge, came to Rome unarmed, looking like beggars. They were welcomed warmly and distributed amongst different houses. Once their wounds healed, many returned home and spoke of the kindness they had received from Rome. Some, however, chose to stay in Rome out of affection for their hosts and the City. They were given a district in which they could live, now called the Tuscan Quarter.

THE TARQUIN QUESTION ENDS

15. Spurius Larcius and Titus Herminius were the next consuls for the next year. Then, after that year, Publius Lucretius and Publius Valerius, also known as Publicola, were next chosen as consuls.

In that year, ambassadors from King Porsena arrived for the final time, discussing the possibility of the Tarquin family's return to power. The Senate didn't give an answer but responded by sending Porsena a delegation of their own members who were held in the highest esteem. While a simple answer could have been provided to Porsena's ambassadors in Rome, the delegation wanted to ensure that the topic would be closed forever. They wanted to prevent any kind of disruption to their mutual goodwill by the king continuing to make requests for the Tarquin family. These requests by Porsena were clearly against the freedom of the Roman people and would never be approved, but they didn't want to deny Porsena anything unless his request would lead to Rome's own downfall.

The delegation from the Senate helped King Porsena understand that the Roman people were no longer under a king, but were free, and would rather welcome enemies than kings. They wished for their City to exist as long as there was freedom. If Porsena wanted Rome to be safe, they asked him to let it be free. The king, humbled, said, "Since you're so determined, I'll not bother you with these matters again, nor will I give false hope to the Tarquin family. Whether they need peace or war, they should look elsewhere for their exile, so that nothing disrupts the peace that you and I have." He followed his kind words with kind actions, returning the remaining hostages and giving back the land of the Veiians, which had been taken in a previous treaty.

Tarquinius and his family, now with no hope of returning to Rome as their king, went to Tusculum to live in exile with his son-in-law, Octavius Mamilius. This ensured the peace between King Porsena and the Romans was maintained.

Chapter 3

HANDLING DEFECTORS (505-502 BC)

505 BC — VICTORY AGAINST THE SABINES

16. MARCUS VALERIUS (BROTHER of Publius Valerius Publicola) and Publius Posthumius were next elected as consuls.

During this year, they successfully waged war against the Sabines and were honored with a triumph back in Rome.

504 BC — THE BEGINNINGS OF APPIUS CLAUDIUS

Having been defeated by the Romans, the Sabines prepared for a larger scale. To confront them, and to prevent any sudden threat from Tusculum (from where they anticipated a war, although it wasn't yet declared), the following year Publius Valerius Publicola, was next elected consul for the fourth time, and Titus Lucretius was elected for the second time.

At this time, conflict arose among the Sabines between those advocating for war and those advocating for peace. This conflict gave the Romans an advantage. Attus Clausus, a Sabine who later would become known as Appius Claudius in Rome, was an advocate for peace. However, he found himself at odds with the Sabine war faction and unable to compete with them. As a result, he defected from Regillum to Rome, bringing with him many *clients*, or freed slaves. They were all granted Roman citizenship rights and land beyond the Anio River. This group was known as the Old Claudian tribe, and it grew with the addition of tribesmen from that region. Appius was elected to the Senate and quickly rose to its highest rank.

Consuls Valerius and Lucretius, with their army, invaded the Sabine territories. They devastated their land and defeated them in battle, weakening the Sabines to the point where they posed no immediate threat. They then returned to Rome in triumph.

503 BC — Defecting Colonies from Rome

The following year, Agrippa Menenius and Publius Posthumius were elected as consuls.

Publius Valerius Publicola, widely recognized as the most capable man in Rome in both peace and war, passed away. Despite his glory, he died impoverished. The City covered his funeral expenses. The women of Rome mourned for him as they had for Brutus, his former colleague.

That same year, two Roman colonies, Pometia and Cora, defected to the Auruncians. The Romans declared war on the Auruncians and defeated their large army who had boldly confronted the consuls at their borders. The entire Auruncian war was then focused on Pometia.

The Romans were so enraged that these two colonies had defected that they didn't stop the slaughter even after the battles ended. They killed more people than they captured, executing all the prisoners. The

Auruncians, in their anger, also didn't spare the three hundred Roman hostages they had taken.

The consuls celebrated another triumph in Rome that year.

502 BC — No Mercy to Defectors

17. The next consuls, Opiter Verginius and Spurius Cassius, initially tried to capture Pometia by force. When that failed, the Romans attempted to build wooden siege equipment to aid in their efforts. However, the Auruncians, driven more by their deep-seated hatred for the consuls than by any real hope of victory, launched a counterattack. They stormed out of Pometia armed with flaming torches, causing fire and destruction wherever they went. They managed to burn down the vineae, a part of the siege equipment, and then killed and injured many of the Romans. They nearly killed one of the consuls, who had been thrown from his horse and badly injured. The identity of this consul isn't specified by historical sources. After this disaster, the Romans returned home. They carried a substantial number of wounded soldiers back, among them the consul, whose condition was critical.

Following a brief period of recovery for the soldiers and a fresh addition of new soldiers and supplies, the consuls returned back to Pometia even angrier than before. This time, the wooden siege equipment had been prebuilt and other war preparations were made ahead of time. The Romans were ascending the walls when Pometia decided to surrender. However, the Romans weren't interested in accepting their surrender this time. In fact, it would have been better for the Pometians to fight, since the outcomes were ultimately the same. They beheaded the Auruncian leaders as if the city had been captured by force. The remaining townsfolk were sold off as slaves. Pometia was razed to the ground and the land was sold.

The consuls obtained a triumph, not so much for the difficulty of the war which they had won, but more for the satisfaction of their revenge.

Chapter 4

TARQUINIUS TRIES AGAIN (501-495 BC)

18. In the following year, Postumus Cominius and Titus Lartius served as consuls.

During a festival in Rome that year, some Sabine youth playfully abducted some prostitutes, leading to a public brawl that nearly escalated into a full-blown battle. This minor incident blew up, eventually inflaming all of Rome and pushing the Romans toward the possibility of a renewed conflict with the Sabines. Adding to their worries was the news that thirty different states had formed an alliance against Rome, spurred on by Octavius Mamilius, the son-in-law of Tarquinius.

THE FIRST DICTATOR

As the City prepared itself for whatever big events might happen, the idea of appointing a dictator was proposed for the first time. However, it's unclear when this happened, who the consuls were at the time, or who was chosen as the first dictator. According to some of the oldest records, Titus Lartius was the first dictator, with Spurius Cassius as his Master of the Horse. They were both men of consular rank, as required by the law for the election of a dictator. This leads me to believe that Titus Lartius, a man of consular rank, was chosen to guide and control the consuls, rather than Manius Valerius, who hadn't yet been a consul.

When the first dictator was appointed in Rome, the sight of the fasces carried before him struck fear into the plebeians, making them more fanatical about obeying orders. There would be no more asking help from a second consul who shared power. There would be no more right to appeal. Obedience mattered, and nothing else. The appointment of a dictator also frightened the Sabines because they believed he was appointed specifically because of them.

The Sabines sent ambassadors to ask for peace, claiming this whole misunderstanding was just youthful escapades. Rome's response was that the actions of young men could be forgiven, but the older men who constantly stirred up fresh wars could not. Negotiations for peace continued and would have been successful if the Sabines had agreed to pay for the war expenses, which they didn't.

War was officially declared against the Sabines, but not acted upon. A mutual standstill between the two parties kept the rest of the year peaceful.

500 BC — AN UNEVENTFUL YEAR

19. In the following year, Servius Sulpicius and Marcus Tullius served as consuls.

However, there were no significant events during their term.

499 BC — BATTLE OF LAKE REGILLUS

The next consuls were Titus Aebutius and Caius Veturius.

During their term, Fidenae was under siege, Crustumeria was captured, and Praeneste switched sides from the Latins to the Romans. A war against the Latins, which had been brewing for several years, could no longer be postponed and it broke out.

Aulus Postumius was appointed as Dictator, and Titus Aebutius served as his Master of the Horse. They led a large army of cavalry and infantry to meet the Latin forces at Lake Regillus, located in the Tusculum territory. Upon hearing that the Tarquins were part of the Latin army, the Romans were filled with anger and could not be stopped. They rushed into battle, fighting with more intensity and bitterness than ever before. The generals weren't only giving strategic orders but jumped into the battle and were actively fighting, as well. In fact, almost all the high-ranking officers from both sides were injured, except for the dictator, Postumius.

As Postumius was rallying the troops on the front line, Tarquinius Superbus, despite his old age, charged at him with great force. During the charge, Tarquinius was struck in his side and had to be rescued by his men.

On the other flank, Aebutius, the Master of the Horse, charged Octavius Mamilius, the Tusculan general and Tarquinius' son-in-law. Mamilius noticed Aebutius charging so he, too, rode at Aebutius full speed. So terrific was the shock when their lances collided with each other that Aebutius' arm was pierced straight through and Mamilius was speared in the breast. He was immediately led off by the Latins into their second line, in the rear. Aebutius, unable to hold a weapon with his wounded arm, retired from the fighting.

Mamilius, ignoring his wound, infused fresh energy into the battle. Seeing that his own men were retreating, he called up a cohort of Roman exiles led by Lucius Tarquinius, the former Roman king's son. Their anger at being banished from their homeland and losing their property fueled them to fight more angrily. For a short time they turned the tide in the battle, and the Romans began to give ground.

20. As the Romans started to retreat, Marcus Valerius, the brother of Publicola, noticed the fiery young Lucius Tarquinius leading his

front line conspicuously, as if he were inviting an attack. Marcus Valerius, inspired by his brother's glory, felt that the family who expelled
the Tarquins should also be credited with their death. He dug the
spurs into his horse and charged, raising his lance. The young Tarquinius evaded the charge by retreating into the exiles' line and, as
Valerius recklessly tried to pursue him, one of these soldiers plunged
a spear through him from behind. Valerius' horse continued running
at full speed despite the fatal wound until the dying Roman, weapons
and armor falling from his body, fell to the ground.

Witnessing a brave soldier fall in such a shocking way, Dictator
Postumius saw his men were now losing the will to fight as the exiles
continued their advance with added strength. In response, he ordered
his personal guard to treat any Roman soldier fleeing the battle as an
enemy. They now had no choice and had to reform the lines instead
of retreat. The Dictator's guard then joined the battle, attacking the
now-tiring exiles with renewed energy and determination, slaughtering many of them.

Another battle broke out between the leading officers on both
sides. General Mamilius, noticing the exiles being surrounded by Dictator Postumius, rushed to the front with some reserve troops. Titus
Herminius, a Roman lieutenant-general, saw him and recognized the
Latin general by his armor and clothing. He attacked Mamilius with
such force that he killed him with a single spear thrust through his
side. However, while stripping the body of armor and weapons, Titus
Herminius, himself, was hit with a spear. He later died back at camp
while his wound was being treated.

The Roman dictator then turned to the cavalry, ordering them to
dismount and join the fight as the foot soldiers were exhausted. They
obeyed, dismounted, and joined the front line, using their shields
for protection. This gave the infantry new courage, seeing the young

nobles sharing the danger with them. The Latins were finally pushed back and retreated. The cavalry was given their horses to chase the enemy, and the infantry followed.

Dictator Postumius, wanting to secure both divine and human help, is said to have promised to build a Temple to Castor and Pollux. He also promised rewards to the first and second soldiers who would enter the enemy's camp. The Romans were so eager that they took the camp with the same energy they had used to defeat the enemy in the field.

This concluded the Battle at Lake Regillus. The Dictator and Master of the Horse returned to the City in triumph.

498-497 BC — SATURN TEMPLE AND SATURNALIA ESTABLISHED

21. Over the next three years, there was neither a stable peace nor an outright war. The consuls during this time were Quintus Cloelius and Titus Lartius, followed by Aulus Sempronius and Marcus Minucius.

During their consulship, a temple was dedicated to the god Saturn, and the Saturnalia was established as a holiday.

496 BC — UNCERTAINTY

Aulus Postumius and Titus Verginius were then elected as consuls.

In some historical accounts, it's suggested that the Battle at Lake Regillus didn't occur until this year. It's also suggested that Aulus Postumius, due to doubts about Verginius' loyalty, resigned from his position as consul and was subsequently appointed as dictator.

The differences in dates and the different arrangements of magistrates in the various historical sources I use make it difficult for me to determine which consuls followed which and what was done in each year. These events, and the people who recorded them, happened so long ago that they're now hidden in the shadows of ancient history.

495 BC — TARQUINIUS DIES

Appius Claudius and Publius Servilius were then elected as consuls.

The last year was notable for the news of Tarquinius' death. He died in Cumae, where he had sought refuge with the tyrant Aristodemus after the decline of the Latins' power. The news of his death was met with joy by both the Senate and the plebeians. However, the senators' satisfaction was excessive, and they began to oppress the plebeians, whom they had previously treated with respect.

In the same year, the colony that King Tarquinius had sent to Signia was replenished by increasing the number of colonists. The number of tribes in Rome was increased to twenty-one. The Temple of Mercury was also dedicated on the fifteenth of May.

PEACE WITH THE LATINS, DISGUST WITH THE VOLSCIANS

22. At the time of the wars against the Latins, the Volscians had been neutral. They were neither at peace with Rome nor at war with it. The Volscians prepared to support the Latins with additional troops, and they would have been successful had Dictator Postumius not acted swiftly to prevent this. His quick actions were aimed at preventing a situation where Romans would have to fight both the Latins and the Volscians simultaneously. Angrily, the Roman consuls led their armies into Volscian territory pre-emptively and surprised the Volscians, who hadn't anticipated any punishment for their intentions. They offered

three-hundred children of their nobility from Cora and Pometia as hostages. Consequently, the Roman legions withdrew without any battle.

Shortly afterward, the Volscians stopped fearing more repercussions and returned back to their usual deceit. They secretly prepared for war again, this time bringing the Hernicians in as allies and sending out ambassadors in all directions to agitate the other Latins into rebellion, as well. However, with the recent defeat at Lake Regillus still on their minds, the Latins instead became enraged and could barely keep from attacking the ambassadors as they suggested taking up arms against the Romans yet again. The Latins, disgusted, arrested the Volscian ambassadors and brought them to Rome. There, they presented them to the consuls and informed them that the Volscians and Hernicians were preparing for war against them. When the matter was referred to the Senate, they were so grateful that they released six-thousand prisoners back to the Latins and approved treaty negotiations, which had previously been almost entirely denied, for next year's incoming magistrates.

The Latins were pleased with these actions, and those who had advocated for this peaceful resolution were highly regarded. They sent a golden crown to the Capitoline Hill as an offering to Jupiter. Along with the ambassadors who brought this offering, a large crowd of formerly enslaved Latin prisoners who had been released came with them and returned to their Roman host families. They visited the homes of those who had kept them during their captivity, expressing thanks for their humane treatment during such a difficult time. They then established friendly relations. Never had the Latin name been more closely tied to the Roman state, either through public or private connections.

Chapter 5

DEBT TURNS CITIZENS INTO SLAVES (495 BC)

23. [NEXT, PUBLIUS SERVILIUS and Appius Claudius were voted in as consuls. — lcw.]

Despite now knowing war with the Volscians was imminent, the City was still torn with internal dissension. The patricians and the plebeians, the commoners, were bitterly hostile to one another, owing mainly to the desperate condition of debtors. The plebeians voiced their grievances loudly, arguing that while they fought as soldiers for freedom and power abroad, they were oppressed and enslaved back at home by their own fellow citizens. They claimed that their freedom was more secure in war than in peace, and that their freedom was safer among enemies than it was among their own people.

THE OLD CENTURION

This discontent grew, and the harsh experiences of one man further inflamed it. An old man, bearing visible scars of all the evils he had suffered, suddenly appeared in the Forum. His clothing was covered with filth, he was thin and emaciated like a corpse, and his unkempt beard and hair made him look like a savage. Despite his appearance, he was recognized by the crowd. They said that he had been a centurion and were able to mention some of the military distinctions which he possessed. He showed them the scars on his chest, proof of his participation in numerous honorable battles.

As they asked him, "Why are you dressed like that? What happened to you?" the small crowd grew into a large assembly. The man explained that he had served in the Sabine war. During this time, his land was ravaged by the enemy, his farm was burned down, his belongings were plundered, and his livestock were slaughtered. A war tax was imposed on him when he was least able to pay it, leading him to incur debt. This debt, increased by interest, first took away his father's and grandfather's farm, then his other properties. Finally, the debt affected his health. His creditor took him not into normal servitude, but into an underground workshop-prison, a living death. He showed his back, marked with fresh whip scars.

Uproar Over Debtor Treatment

The sight and story in the Forum caused an uproar. Outcry spread throughout the City. Those currently in bondage for debt and those who had been released rushed into the streets, sharing their stories and pleading for the people's protection. They found willing supporters everywhere as they ran through the streets to the Forum, shouting loudly.

Some senators who were in the Forum at the time found themselves in a dangerous situation. The consuls, Publius Servilius and Appius Claudius, quickly intervened to calm the situation. The crowd turned to them, showing their chains and the signs of their misery. Former soldiers taunted the consuls with their own military achievements and demanded that they convene the Senate. They surrounded the senate-house, determined to witness and direct the public discussions. Only a few senators, who happened to be nearby, joined the consuls.

Fear kept the rest away from the Forum and the senate-house, and the Senate could not act due to the lack of members.

The people began to believe that their demands were being ignored and their grievances weren't being addressed. They thought that the absent senators were deliberately obstructing the process and accused the consuls of mocking their suffering. The situation had escalated to the point where even the authority of the consuls could barely control the people's rage.

The senators, unsure whether they were in greater danger by staying home or going in, finally attended the Senate. However, even with enough people to conduct business, there was disagreement among the senators and between the consuls themselves. Appius Claudius, a hot-headed man, believed that the consuls' authority could resolve the issue by arresting and making an example of one or two people and this would calm the rest. Servilius, more moderate, thought it would be safer and easier to appease the people rather than confront them directly.

TWO DIFFERENT VIEWS OF WAR

24. Amid these debates, a more serious threat emerged. A Latin messenger arrived in Rome at full speed, bringing the alarming news that the Volscian army was now advancing to attack the City. This report had a different impact on the patricians and the plebeians due to the anger that had divided the state. The plebeians were overjoyed, believing that the gods were punishing the tyranny of the patricians. They encouraged each other not to enlist, arguing that it was better for all to perish together than for them to die alone. Patricians, they said, should put on their armor and serve as soldiers! They should face the dangers of war, as they were the ones who profited from it the most!

The Senate, however, was filled with fear and confusion because now there were threats from both their own people as well as the enemy. They pleaded with Consul Servilius, known for his conciliatory nature, to save the state from these threats. The consul adjourned the Senate and addressed the people. The Senate was concerned about the people's interests, he said. However, the imminent threat of war had interrupted their deliberations. He argued that it was dishonorable for the plebeians to refuse to take up arms for their country until they had been rewarded with legislation. It was also dishonorable, he argued, for the senators to be forced to pass hastily made resolutions out of fear. Instead, they should be allowed to pass these resolutions out of their own free will.

To prove to the people that they could put their trust in him, the consul issued an edict stating that no Roman citizen shall be kept in chains and be prevented from enlisting for military service. He also declared that no one should seize or sell a soldier's possessions while he was in the camp, nor harass his children or grandchildren. Upon hearing this edict, the debtors who were present in the Forum immediately enlisted. Enslaved debtors from all over the City, now allowed to leave their conditions behind, rushed to the Forum to take the oath to serve. This resulted in a flood of enlistees who showed as much bravery and energy in the Volscian war as the others.

THE DEBTOR ARMY

The consul then led his army against the enemy, setting up camp a short distance away from them.

25. The Volscians were still under the impression that there was severe disagreement among the Romans. The next night, they tried to infiltrate the Romans' camp, hoping that the darkness would en-

courage desertions and betrayals. However, the guards on duty spotted them. The army was alerted and, upon receiving the alarm, the soldiers rushed to their arms. This thwarted the Volscians' plan and both armies spent the rest of the night sleeping.

At dawn, the Volscians filled the trenches and launched an attack on the rampart. As fortifications were being torn down from all sides, Consul Servilius waited to give the signal despite the cries from all around. The debtors were especially hungry for battle. He held back to gauge the soldiers' morale. When their eagerness for battle was evident, he finally gave the signal to charge. The soldiers, wild for battle, were let loose on the enemy. The enemy was defeated at the very first charge. As the enemy retreated, they were pursued as long as the Roman infantry could keep up. The cavalry then took over, driving them in panic all the way back to their camp. As soldiers continued to arrive and surround the camp, the Volscians abandoned it and fled. Once the camp was surrounded, the Romans captured and looted it. The next day, the legions were led to Pometia, where the enemy had retreated. The town was captured within a few days and was given up to be looted. This provided some relief to the impoverished soldiers.

The consul, with great honor, led his victorious army back to Rome. As they were leaving for Rome, representatives from the Volscians at Ecetra approached him. They were fearful for their state after the capture of Pometia. The Senate granted them peace, but some of their land was seized.

26. Immediately after this had happened, news came in throughout the City that the Sabine army had reached the Anio river, plundering the land and setting farmhouses on fire after they had stolen all their contents. Aulus Postumius, who had previously served as a dictator during the Latin war, was quickly dispatched to confront them, leading the cavalry. Consul Servilius followed him, leading a select group

of infantry. The cavalry managed to eliminate most of the stragglers who had fallen behind the Sabine army, and the full Sabine legion didn't put up any resistance against the infantry when they finally caught up with them. The Sabines were too exhausted from their march and their nighttime looting to put up a fight. Many of them had overindulged in food and wine from the farms, so they barely had enough energy to flee. The Sabine conflict was thus reported and concluded in a single night.

The next day, as everyone had hoped that the wars had concluded and that peace was now assured everywhere, ambassadors from the Auruncians arrived at the Senate. The Auruncians would now declare war, they said, unless Roman troops were pulled out from Volscian territory. The full Auruncian army had left their home for Rome at the same time as the ambassadors. Then, news came in that the army was spotted not far from Aricia. This caused such a commotion among the Romans that there was no time to debate the matter in the Senate, nor could the Romans, while arming themselves, give a peaceful response to those who were marching toward Rome. So, the Romans marched to meet them in Aricia. The two armies engaged not far from that town, ending the war in a single battle.

MIDDLE OF THE ROAD LEADERSHIP FAILS

27. After this, the Auruncians were defeated. The Roman soldiers, who had won many wars in a short time, now waited for the promises of Consul Servilius and the Senate to be fulfilled. However, Appius Claudius, known for his innate love of tyranny and his desire to discredit his colleague, issued harsh decrees about borrowed money.

People who had previously been imprisoned were handed back over to their creditors. Even worse, new citizens were now also taken into custody. When a soldier was affected by this, he would appeal to Consul Servilius, and a crowd would gather around him. They reminded him of his promises and their contributions to the wars, showing him their battle scars. Bring the matter to the Senate, they urged. Or, as consul, help his fellow citizens. Or, as a general, be there for his soldiers.

Servilius was indecisive. He was moved by their pleas, but the current political situation made him delay deciding what to do. His colleague had the steadfast support of the entire patrician class. And so, by trying to play both sides, he didn't escape the anger of the people nor did he win the favor of the senators. The senators saw him as a weak popularity-seeker, and the people saw him as a dishonest trickster. It soon became clear that he was as disliked as Appius Claudius.

REBELLION AGAINST PATRICIAN LEADERS

A disagreement arose between the consuls about which of them should dedicate the Temple of Mercury. The Senate left the decision to the people. Whomever the people chose would preside over the market, form a guild of merchants, and perform functions in the presence of the Pontifex Maximus. The people chose Marcus Laetorius, a senior centurion of the first rank, a man of lower status who was widely seen as unqualified for such an important job. The people chose the centurion solely to humiliate the consuls and, indeed, both the consuls and the senators were incensed.

However, the people didn't relent. They threw themselves into the struggle, erupting with self-determination when they understood that their leaders wouldn't help them. The plebeians took matters into their own hands. Whenever they saw a debtor being taken to court, they gathered around and shouted, creating an uproar. The consul's sentence could not be heard over the noise, and, even when it could, no one obeyed the sentence when it was announced. Violence became commonplace. The fear and danger experienced by debtors was now transferred over to the creditors, who were singled out by the mob and beaten up in front of the consul.

On top of this, fear of a war with the Sabines spread. However, when a draft was announced, no one enlisted. Appius Claudius was livid. He accused Servilius of betraying the republic by seeking fame and publicity while not doing what he should have been doing: passing judgment against the debtors and raising troops for the draft. However, he said, the state wasn't lost. The senators' authority hadn't been abandoned. He, himself, single-handedly, would champion his own sovereignty and that of the senators.

When the daily mob of unruly people gathered around him again, this time he ordered the arrest of a man who appeared to be the ringleader. As the lictors were dragging the man away, he cried out for an appeal. The consul wouldn't have allowed the appeal, for he was quite confident how the people would decide, if not for the prudent advice of the senators around him. Appius Claudius, the proud man that he was, was more than prepared to be hated by the people.

The situation became more serious every day, not only through open protests but, what was far more dangerous, through secret meetings and plotting by the plebeians. Eventually, the consuls, who were universally hated by the plebeians, left office. Servilius was equally hated by both sides and Appius Claudius was hated by the plebeians but praised by the senators.

Chapter 6
THE FIRST TRIBUNES
(494 BC)

28. NEXT, AULUS VERGINIUS and Titus Veturius became consuls.

The plebeians, unsure of what kind of leaders they would be, started holding secret meetings at night. Some met on the Esquiline Hill, others on the Aventine Hill. They did this to avoid making rushed decisions and pronouncements in the Forum. The consuls saw this as a dangerous act, as it was, and made a formal report to the Senate.

A THOUSAND LITTLE COUNCILS AND ASSEMBLIES

Any hope for rational discussion was crushed as the Senate degenerated into shouting, indignant about having to deal with an unsavory issue that, in their minds, the consuls should have already handled by now. They already had the power to resolve it, so what was the problem? "If there were real leadership in the republic," it was said, "there would only be one single council in Rome and no meetings beyond that. Now, the republic is divided into a thousand little councils and assemblies, some on the Esquiline Hill, others on the Aventine Hill. A man like Appius Claudius would have easily broken up these private meetings." The consuls, now having been publicly reprimanded, continued to ask the senators what they should do. They wanted to give the issue the attention and energy that the senators wanted. Accordingly, the Senate passed a decree to start the draft as quickly as possible, as the plebeians were becoming unruly due to lack of work.

After the meeting, the consuls ascended the tribunal and summoned the young men of Rome who would be drafted, by their names. No one responded. Instead, the plebeians gathered around the consuls and said they wouldn't fight until the government kept its promises. They wanted their rights restored so that they were fighting for their country and their fellow citizens, not for tyrannical leaders. The consuls understood the Senate's decree to begin the draft, but none of the senators who had spoken so boldly in the Senate were there to help them deal with the public's anger. The consuls felt a fierce battle with the plebeians was imminent. The consuls decided to return to the Senate and consult them a second time. This time, the younger senators rushed from their seats to confront the consuls, telling them to resign if they could not handle their duties.

As in the Forum, So Too in the Senate

29. Having had enough of trying to coerce the plebeians on the one hand and persuading the Senate to adopt a milder course on the other, the consuls finally told the Senate, "Honorable Senators, we want to warn you that a significant disturbance is imminent. We ask those who criticize us the harshest for being cowardly to help us raise the draft to get needed soldiers. We will act according to the decision of the bravest among you, if that is what you wish."

The consuls returned to their platform. They deliberately called out the name of one of the most rebellious people, one whom they could physically see, to be summoned for the draft. The man remained silent. Accordingly, the consuls sent a lictor to get him. The lictor was subsequently pushed back by the mob. The senators who were with the consuls were outraged by such blatant disrespect by the plebeians. They rushed from the platform to try to help the lictor. The mob then dropped their hostility toward the lictor, who was only being blocked from arresting the man, and aimed all of their anger toward the senators. The consuls intervened and prevented a riot from happening. No stones or weapons had been used, so there was more heated rhetoric and shouting than physical injury done.

The Senate was summoned and assembled in disorder. Those who had been roughly handled by the mob demanded an investigation, and the most aggressive members expressed their views as much through shouting and noise as through their votes. Finally, when their anger had cooled, the consuls scolded them for being as out of control in the Senate as it was in the Forum. Then, debate began in an orderly manner. There were three different policies advocated:

Publius Verginius didn't generalize the issue. He suggested that they should only consider reinstating the freedom of those who, trusting in the promises made by former consul Publius Servilius, had fought in the wars against the Volscians, Auruncans, and Sabines.

Titus Largius believed that the time had passed to reward only those who had served. He said that all the plebeians were in debt, and the problem could not be solved unless steps were taken for everyone, universally. He also said that if different groups were treated differently, it would only increase divisions rather than resolve them.

Appius Claudius, by nature merciless and brutal, had become even angrier from his hatred toward the plebeians on one hand and the praises from senators on the other. He said that the problems they were having weren't due to hardship, but to lawlessness. The plebeians were gathering not because of actual misery, but because they felt entitled. They were motivated by celebrating antisocial behavior more than anything else. The right to appeal, he argued, was the root cause of this serious problem. The consuls had only threats, not actual authority, because those who were part of a crime were allowed to appeal to people who were also criminals. "Let's appoint a Dictator from whom there is no appeal. This insanity which is setting everything on fire will immediately die down. I'd like to see anyone strike a lictor when he knows that his own life will be in the hands of the person whose authority he has just insulted!"

30. The reaction was mixed. Many senators thought Appius Claudius' motion was cruel and monstrous, which it actually was. On the other hand, the views of Publius Verginius and Titus Largius were seen as risky because of the precedent they set. Largius' opinion was particularly concerning because it would destroy trust. Verginius' opinion was considered the most balanced, a good middle ground between the other two. However, due to political divisions and personal interests, which have interfered and will always interfere with public policy, Appius' view ultimately won out. He was very close to being made dictator, himself. This move would have alienated the plebeians at a time when the Volscians, Aequians, and Sabines were all in arms together. However, the consuls and older senators ensured that the powerful position of dictator was given to a moderate man, Manius Valerius.

The plebeians, even though they knew this official was chosen against their interests, were also not afraid of him or his family. They knew they had the right to appeal under the very same laws that his brother passed. An edict from Dictator Valerius followed, similar to one issued by Consul Servilius, which reassured them. The plebeians now felt as if they could trust the man and the authority of his position, so they stopped protesting and enlisted in the army. Ten legions were formed, the largest army ever. Each consul led three legions, and Dictator Valerius led four. The war could not be delayed any longer.

War with the Volscians: Standing Still

The Aequians had invaded Latin territory, and the Latin envoys asked the Senate for help or permission to arm themselves. The Senate decided it was safer to defend the Latins without arming them, so Consul Veturius and his legions were sent to help. This stopped the invasions. The Aequians retreated from the plains to high in the mountains, relying on the terrain rather than their weapons to protect them.

The other consul, Verginius, advanced against the Volscians. To speed the process, he ransacked their fields with the idea of forcing them to move their camp nearer to his and bring on an engagement. The two armies stood facing each other, in front of their respective ramparts, on the level space between the camps. The Volscians had considerably more soldiers and, accordingly, showed their contempt for their foe by charging recklessly into battle toward the Romans. However, the Roman consul ordered his army motionless and forbade them from shouting any battle cries. He ordered them to stand with their spears fixed in the ground and, when the enemy came within close range, to spring forward and use their swords.

The Volscians finally arrived at the Roman lines, now tired with their running and their shouting, and tried to attack, thinking that the Romans were frozen with fear. However, when they felt the strength of the counterattack and saw the swords flashing before them, they retreated in confusion just as if they had been caught in an ambush. As they had been running so fast and so carelessly into battle, they didn't have the strength to flee. The Romans, on the other hand, since at the beginning of the battle they had remained quietly standing, were fresh and vigorous. They easily overtook the exhausted Volscians, took their camp, and pursued them all the way to Velitrae, the victors and the vanquished bursting headfirst into the city. More blood was shed there in the city than in the battle, with only a few Volscians spared after they threw down their weapons and surrendered.

APPALLED AT ROMAN AUDACITY

31. While events were unfolding among the Volscians, Dictator Valerius, and his legions entered Sabine territory, where the most serious part of the war was. There, he defeated and chased the Sabines out of their camp. The Dictator used his cavalry to disrupt the enemy's center line, as it was weak due to the line's wings being overextended. The infantry attacked in this scattered chaos, capturing their camp and ending the war in one move. This battle was the most notable of its time, second only to the Battle of Lake Regillus. Dictator Valerius was celebrated with a triumphant return to the City. In addition to the usual honors, he and his descendants were given a special place in the Circus Maximus to watch the public games, and a ceremonial curule chair was placed there.

Meanwhile, as the lands of Velitrae were taken from the defeated Volscians, colonists from the City were sent to establish a colony there.

Soon after, there was a clash with the Aequians. Consul Veturius was reluctant to pursue this battle because the terrain was unfavorable, but the soldiers believed that the war was being deliberately prolonged so that the Dictator's term of office would expire before they returned home and his promises wouldn't be carried out. Veturius agreed to a chaotic trek up the hill. However, this risky move was successful due to the enemy's cowardice. The Aequians, shocked at watching how the Romans were attempting such an audacious maneuver on their strategically-position camp at the top, slid down the other side of the hill and fled into the valley below. The Romans found plenty of spoils in the camp, and victory was achieved without bloodshed.

THE DICTATOR DEFENDS DEBTOR SOLDIERS

Despite three military successes, both the senators and the plebeians were still anxious about their internal conflicts. The creditors possessed such influence and had maneuvered so skillfully that they rendered the people and even the Dictator, himself, powerless. After Consul Veturius had returned, Dictator Valerius introduced a proposal, as the very first business of the Senate, on behalf of the debtor soldiers who had brought victory to Rome. He asked that they make a decision about how Rome would handle these debtors. His proposal was rejected.

The Dictator responded to the Senate, "To you all, I'm not acceptable as an advocate of peace. Rest assured that you'll soon wish that the Roman plebeians had champions like me. As far as I'm concerned, I'll no longer encourage my fellow citizens in their hope. Nor will I be a dictator in vain. Internal dissensions and foreign wars have made this office necessary to the City. Peace has now been secured abroad, but, at home, it has been made impossible. I'd rather witness this mutiny as a private citizen than as dictator." After these words, Marcus Valerius resigned his dictatorship and left the Senate.

Even though Valerius wasn't successful in persuading the Senate, it didn't matter. When the plebeians heard that he had resigned his office out of indignation at their treatment, they escorted him back home and praised him along the way, just as if he were.

THE SOLDIERS SECEDE

32. The senators were now gripped by fear. If the army would be disbanded, the secret meetings and plots of the plebeians would start again. Although the army had been assembled by the Dictator, the soldiers were still bound by their oath to obey the consuls. At least, this is what the senators believed. Using the excuse of renewed hostilities with the Aequians, they ordered the legions to leave the City. This accelerated the rebellion. It's said that, initially, there were plans to kill the consuls so the soldiers could be released from their oath. However, they learned that a criminal act could not dissolve a religious obligation.

Following the advice of Lucius Sicinius Vellutus, the soldiers left without the consuls' permission and retreated to the Sacred Mount, beyond the Anio river, three miles from the City. This version of events is more widely accepted than Piso's account, which claims the secession was made to the Aventine Hill. There, without a leader, the legions built and fortified a camp with a rampart and a trench. They remained peaceful, taking only what was necessary for survival, and didn't attack or get attacked for several days.

Meanwhile, the City was in a state of panic and business came to a halt. The plebeians left inside the City feared the senators, while the senators feared the plebeians, unsure whether it was better for them to stay or leave. How long the seceded group would remain peaceful? What would happen if a foreign war broke out during this time? The patricians saw their only hope was in the unity of the citizens and decided to restore it by any means necessary.

The consuls chose Menenius Agrippa to be their ambassador, a popular man who was well-liked by the plebeians. Agrippa was born a plebeian and was widely viewed as one of them. He was allowed into the legions' camp where he told the following story in an old-fashioned and crude style:

"Once upon a time, the parts of the human body didn't work together as they do now. Each part had its own plan and language. The other parts were angry that they worked hard to provide for the belly, which did nothing but enjoy the pleasures they provided. They conspired to starve the belly by refusing to eat. However, this only led to the entire body becoming extremely weak. It became clear that the belly wasn't lazy, but rather, it distributed nourishment to all parts of the body. This blood, which we live and gain strength from, is sent to the veins after the food is digested." By comparing the rebellion of the body parts to the plebeians' resentment towards the patricians, he managed to influence the crowd.

THE FIRST TRIBUNES

33. The process of reconciliation began. Eventually, they agreed upon a compromise with the following terms: the plebeians would have their own leaders with unbreakable rights. These leaders would have the authority to provide help against actions by the consuls. Finally, no patrician would be allowed to hold this position.

As a result, two tribunes of the plebeians were appointed, Caius Licinius and Lucius Albinus. They chose three colleagues to join them. It's known that Lucius Sicinius, the instigator of the rebellion, was one of them, but the identities of the other two are uncertain. Some believe that only two plebeian tribunes were elected on the Sacred Mount, and that the sacred law of inviolability was passed there.

Chapter 7

FAMINE (493-491 BC)

DURING THE PLEBEIANS' SECESSION, Spurius Cassius and Postumus Cominius began their consulship. Under their leadership, a treaty with the Latin states was finalized. One of the consuls stayed in Rome while the other was sent to the Volscian War. He defeated and chased away the Volscians of Antium, driving them into the town of Longula, where he took control of the town. He then captured Polusca, another Volscian town, and launched an attack on Corioli with his entire force.

493 BC — CNAEUS MARCIUS "CORIOLANUS"

Among the most distinguished of the young soldiers in the camp was Cnaeus Marcius, who was known for his intelligence and bravery. Marcius later earned the nickname Coriolanus for his bravery at Corioli.

During the siege of Corioli, the Romans had been concentrating on the townspeople imprisoned inside its walls. The Romans had felt that they had everything under control and hadn't anticipated any external threats. Suddenly, Volscian legions from Antium appeared, surprising them, and immediately attacked. Soldiers from Corioli then burst from the city's gates to attack the Romans.

As this happened, Marcius was on watch. He and a carefully chosen group of soldiers not only stopped the soldiers from Corioli from spilling out but also forced their way through the open gate. After killing many people in the area of the city closest to them, Marcius grabbed a firebrand and threw it at the buildings that could be seen over the city walls. The cries of the townspeople and the wailing of the women and children increased the Romans' courage. It crushed the Volscians because they had come to help a defend a city that was now in the hands of their enemies. As a result, the Volscians of Antium were defeated, and the town of Corioli was captured. Marcius' fame overshadowed Consul Cominius' reputation so much that if it weren't for the treaty with the Latins, which Spurius Cassius alone concluded because his colleague was absent, people would have forgotten that Postumus Cominius had led the war against the Volscians.

That same year, Agrippa Menenius, a man loved by both senators and plebeians, died. He was even more beloved by the plebeians after the secession. Despite his role in restoring harmony among his countrymen and bringing the plebeians secessionists back to the City, he lacked the funds for his funeral. The people buried him, each contributing a small amount to cover the costs.

492 BC — NEGOTIATING FOR FOOD

34. Titus Geganius and Publius Minutius were elected as the next consuls.

In this year, undisturbed by war and civic dissent, the City was attacked by another much more serious evil: famine. First, there was a shortage of food, caused by fields remaining uncultivated during the secession. Then, there was a widespread, protracted starvation such as what happens during a siege. It would have led to the deaths of the slaves in any case, and probably the plebeians would have died, had the consuls not provided for the emergency by sending men in various directions to buy grain. They went not just to the Etruscans on the coast to the right of Ostia and through the Volscians along the coast on the left as far as Cumae, but also as far away as Sicily.

The state's strained relations with its neighbors nearby forced it to seek help from distant lands, but they also had problems abroad. When corn was bought at Cumae, the Romans' ships were seized by Aristodemus, the local tyrant who was the heir to the Tarquins. In the Volsci and Pomptine district, they not only refused, but the lives of the people sent to buy grain were in danger because of the hostile local population. In the end, it was negotiated that grain from the Etruscans would come to Rome via the Tiber and this helped sustain the people.

During this food shortage, the City could have been further troubled by war from the Volscians if a severe disease hadn't struck them just as they were preparing for war. The disease scared the Volscians and even after it subsided, they were so ravaged by it that they were still fearful. The Romans took advantage of this and increased their colonists at Velitrae and sent a new colony to the mountains of Norba to act as a stronghold in the Pomptine district.

491 BC — "LET THEM FIGHT WITHOUT FOOD"

In the consulship of Marcus Minucius and Aulus Sempronius, a large amount of grain was imported from Sicily and the Senate debated on the price it should be sold to the plebeians. Many thought that the time had come for the plebeians to be suppressed and to recover the rights which had been taken from the Senate by secession and force.

Coriolanus, who was against the power of the plebeian tribunes, addressed his fellow senators: "If they want their grain at the old price, let them restore the old rights of the senators! Why do I see plebeian magistrates? Why do I see Sicinius in power? After being forced to submission, then ransomed as it were from thieves, am I to endure these indignities a moment longer than I can help? Am I, who could not put up with Tarquinius as king, to now put up with Sicinius? Let him secede now! Let him call out his plebeians! The way lies open to the Sacred Mount and to other hills. Let them seize the grain from our fields as they did three years ago! Let them enjoy the scarcity which, in their madness, they have caused! I'll venture to say that after they have been tamed by these sufferings, they would rather work as laborers in the fields, themselves, rather than prevent the fields from being cultivated by armed secession."

It isn't easy to say whether this should have been done, but it seems possible to me that the senators could have lowered the price of grain in exchange for formally ending the power of the plebeian tribunes and all the restrictions imposed on the Senate against their will.

ATTACKED BY STARVATION

35. The Senate found the proposal too severe, and it nearly provoked the plebeians to take up arms in their frustration.

The plebeians felt as though they were being attacked with starvation, as if they were enemies. They believed they were being cheated out of food and sustenance and saw the foreign grain, their only unexpected source of support, being snatched from their mouths. They also felt this would continue until the plebeian tribunes were handed over in chains to Cnaeus Marcius Coriolanus, unless he satisfied his anger on the backs of the Roman plebeians. They saw him as a new executioner who ordered them to die or become slaves.

As Coriolanus left the Senate, he would have been attacked if the plebeian tribunes hadn't quickly set a date for his trial. This action calmed their anger, as everyone saw themselves as the judge and the decision-maker of the life and death of their enemy. At first Coriolanus contemptuously listened to the threats of the plebeian tribunes, reminding them that their role was to provide aid, not punishment, and that they were representatives of the plebeians, not the patricians.

However, the plebeians were so angry that the senators felt they had to protect themselves and sacrifice one of their own to appease them. Despite the plebeians' fury, the patricians withstood the anger and used their individual and collective powers by trying to disrupt the proceedings, placing their clients in various places to discourage individuals from attending the meetings and councils. But they were then ordered to proceed. Gathering in a body—as if all the senators were guilty—they came forward, prayerfully pleading with the plebeians. If the plebeians wouldn't acquit an innocent man, they asked, could they then pardon this single citizen, this senator, whom they might think guilty? However, when Coriolanus didn't attend the trial, the plebeians' anger prevailed and wouldn't let the matter go.

Coriolanus was found guilty in his absence and went into exile to the Volscians, uttering threats against his homeland and considering Rome to be an enemy. The Volscians welcomed him and treated him increasingly well as his resentment towards his countrymen became more apparent to them.

He stayed with Attius Tullius, the leading man of the Volscian people and a long-time enemy of the Romans. Both Coriolanus and Attius Tullius, one driven by old animosity and the other by recent resentment, planned a war against Rome. They didn't immediately believe that their people could be persuaded to take up arms, given their many unsuccessful attempts in the past. Given the loss of so many young men in the frequent wars between the Volscians and also in a recent plague, the morale of the Volscians was low. The two men decided they needed to use deception to reignite the Volscian animosity, now dulled with time, to provoke them with a new cause for anger.

Chapter 8

DECEPTION AT THE GREAT GAMES (489-487 BC)

36. IN ROME, PLANS were underway to repeat the Great Games.

The reason for repeating the games was that during the morning before the previous games, a family head had punished his slave by putting a cattle yoke on him, forcing him through the middle of the Circus Maximus while beating him before the performance had started. The games then began, as if this event had no religious significance.

A MESSAGE FROM JUPITER

However, not long after, a plebeian named Titus Latinius had a dream where Jupiter seemed to tell him that he was displeased with the person who had performed before the games. He warned that unless the games were redone on a grand scale, the City would be in danger. He instructed Latinius to relay this message to the consuls. Although he was somewhat superstitious, Latinius' respect for the authority of the magistrates overpowered his religious fear. He was worried that, if it weren't true, he would become a joke among the people.

This hesitation proved costly, as he lost his son within a few days. To remove any doubt about the cause of this tragedy, the same apparition appeared to him again. It seemed to ask him if he had received enough punishment for his disregard of the deity and warned of a heavier punishment unless he immediately delivered the message to the consuls. Despite the situation becoming more urgent, Latinius continued to hesitate and delay. He was then struck by partial paralysis. This finally awakened him to the gods' anger.

Exhausted by his past sufferings and the threats of more to come, he called a meeting of his friends and told them everything he had seen and heard, including Jupiter's repeated appearances in his dreams and the divine threats being proven true by his own misfortunes. With the unanimous agreement of everyone at the meeting, he was carried in a litter to the consuls in the Forum. From there, he was taken to the Senate, where he relayed the same information to the senators. To everyone's astonishment, another miracle occurred. Latinius, who had been carried into the Senate because he was unable to use any of his limbs, is said to have walked home on his own after he had fulfilled his duty.

CORIOLANUS AND TULLIUS' PLOT

37. The Senate decided that the Great Games should be held on the largest scale possible. A large number of Volscians attended these games, following the advice of Attius Tullius, the Volscian leader. Before the games began, Tullius, who had plotted this scheme ahead of time with Coriolanus, approached the consuls. He informed them that he wanted to discuss private matters concerning the state. All witnesses were ordered to be removed so that they could speak in private.

Once all witnesses were gone, Tullius stated, "I'm hesitant to speak badly about my fellow Volscian countrymen. However, I'm not here to accuse them of any wrongdoing, but to prevent them from committing any wrongdoing. Our people are more unpredictable than I'd like. We have become this way through many misfortunes; we're still standing, not because of our own merits, but because of your patience. A large crowd of Volscians is currently here. The games are underway; the City is focused on the show. I remember what happened in this City during a similar event by the Sabine youth and I fear that something reckless and impulsive may occur. I thought it was necessary to inform you, consuls, about these concerns. As for me, I've decided to return home immediately, so that I'm not influenced by any harmful words or actions."

After saying this, he left. When the consuls presented the matter to the Senate, the credibility of the source, rather than the evidence, persuaded them to take unnecessary precautions. The Senate passed a decree that all Volscians should leave the City immediately, and messengers were sent in various directions to order them to leave before nightfall.

Initially, the Volscians were filled with fear as they rushed to their accommodations to gather their belongings. However, as they were on the way home, fear turned into resentment. Why were they expelled from the games? Were they criminals or people unfit for society? It was a time of festival, and they were being excluded from an event where, in a way, men and gods come together.

TULLIUS AGITATES THE RETURNING VOLSCIANS

38. As they moved forward, leaving Rome in a nearly unbroken stream, the Volscian general Tullius had already left Rome and arrived at the head of the Ferentinum Road. He greeted each of the Volscian leaders as they arrived with their groups, asking questions and expressing his outrage. Their outrage reflected his own. He guided those who

felt the same - who, in turn, guided their groups - into a nearby field off the road. There, he began a speech as if it were a public address:

Tullius said, "Even if you were to forget the past wrongs done to the Roman people and the disasters that fell upon the Volscian nation, how can you tolerate the insult given to you today when they began their games by mocking us? Didn't you feel that they were celebrating a victory over you? That you, when leaving, were a spectacle for all to see? To citizens? To foreigners? And to so many neighboring states? That your wives and your children were put on display for all to see? What do you think those who heard the messengers' announcements felt about us? What about those who saw us picking up and leaving? Or, those who encountered our shameful procession home? What else could they think, except that we're marked by some terrible crime that would taint the games and provoke the gods' displeasure? This is the reason, in their minds, why we were banished from their company and gatherings."

"Does it not occur to you that we're alive only because we left quickly? That is, if this can even be called leaving and not what it really was: fleeing. Don't you see this as a city of enemies, where if you had stayed even one more day, you would have all been killed? War has been declared on you! It'll be a great misfortune for those who declared it, if you are men!"

Already filled with resentment and inflamed even more by this speech, they each went back home, bringing the anger back to their own townspeople who also became outraged. In no time, the entire Volscian nation was livid, ready to rise up in revolt against Rome.

GENERALS OVER ARMIES

39. The Volscian generals unanimously chosen for the war were Attius Tullius and Cnaeus Marcius Coriolanus. They placed their greatest hope in Coriolanus. He didn't let them down, proving that the strength of Rome lay more in its generals than its army.

He led his troops to Circeii, drove out the Roman colonists, and gave the city back to the Volscians as a free city. Coriolanus then moved across the country, taking from the Romans their newly won towns of Satricum, Longula, Polusca, and Corioli, [which he, himself, had recently captured for the Romans]. He recaptured Lavinium and using back roads on the Latin Way, took Corbio, Vitellia, Trebia, Labici, and Pedum. Finally, he marched from Pedum to Rome, setting up his camp at the Cluilian Trenches five miles from the City. From there, he raided the Roman territory, but he sent guards with the raiders to make sure the lands of the patricians weren't touched.

This could have been because Coriolanus was angry with the plebeians, or because, strategically, he wanted to cause conflict between the senators and the plebeians. The conflict would certainly have arisen since the plebeian tribunes were stirring up the plebeians against Rome's leaders, but fear of the enemy kept them united even though they continued to be suspicious and hostile with one another. The only disagreement was that the Senate and consuls wanted to use on military force, while the plebeians wanted to avoid war.

488 BC — STRONGER, NOT WEAKER, BY EXILE

Spurius Nautius and Sextus Furius were voted in as the next consuls.

In this year, the consuls were organizing the legions and setting up guards along the walls and other strategic points when a large crowd demanding peace scared them with loud protests. They were then forced to call a Senate meeting to discuss sending Roman ambassadors to Coriolanus. The Senate agreed to this when they saw that the plebeians' morale was fading.

Ambassadors were sent to Coriolanus to discuss peace, but they returned with a harsh response from him: if the territory taken by the Romans were restored to the Volscians, the question of peace could be discussed. However, if they wished to keep the land and enjoy the spoils of war without fighting, he hadn't forgotten the wrongs inflicted upon him by the Romans nor the kindness shown by the Volscians who were now his hosts. He would make it clear that his spirit had been strengthened, not broken, by being exiled.

When the same ambassadors were sent back a second time, they weren't allowed into the camp. It's said that the priests, dressed in their ceremonial robes, also went to the enemy's camp to plead for peace, but they had no more influence on him than the ambassadors.

"Am I an Enemy or a Mother?"

40. The married women of Rome went to the home of Veturia, the mother of Coriolanus, and his wife, Volumnia. It's unclear to me whether this was due to a public decision or from the women's fear. Regardless, they succeeded in their plan for both Veturia, an elderly woman, and Volumnia to take the two young sons of Coriolanus and enter the enemy camp. As the men were powerless to protect the City by their weapons, the women desired to do so by their tears and prayers.

Upon their arrival at the camp, Coriolanus was informed of an immense number of women standing nearby. Being unmoved by the state's ambassadors and the priests' religious appeals, he was even more resistant to the women's tears. However, when one of his friends recognized his mother, Veturia, standing out due to her sorrow, he pointed her out to Coriolanus. "Unless my eyes are deceiving me," he said, "your mother is here along with your wife and children."

Coriolanus, shocked, rushed to embrace his mother. But Veturia, instead of accepting his warm welcome, angrily spoke to him:

"Before I accept your hug, are you my enemy or are you my son? Am I a prisoner of war in your camp or am I your mother? Is it this to which long life and an unhappy old age have brought me, that I should see you both exiled and then an enemy?"

"Could you bring yourself to destroy and plunder the City which gave you life and raised you? Could you not release that anger, no matter how hostile you felt when you came, as you passed the boundary to come here? Didn't you think to yourself, 'Within these walls are my home and my gods, my mother, my wife, and my children' as the City stood right in front of your eyes?"

"For me, had I not been a mother, Rome would now not be besieged! If I had no son, I'd have died a free woman, in a free land! I can't suffer anything worse that would be more disgraceful to you or more miserable for myself than what I'm suffering now. I'm deeply sorrowful, but my own sorrows will soon be over. The next generation of young people will be the ones killed or enslaved if you continue what you began."

This speech, the embraces of his wife and children, and the tears of the Roman women that accompanied them were too much. Coriolanus' resolve was broken and he embraced his family.

He sent everyone away and moved his forces away from the City. After withdrawing from Roman territory, it's poetically said that Coriolanus died beneath the resentment that this act caused, however, his actual cause of his death varies among different sources. According to Fabius, the most ancient author, Coriolanus lived until an old age and would say, in his advanced age, that exile was far worse for an old man.

The men of Rome praised the women for their actions, and a temple was built in honor of the female *Fortuna Muliebris*, goddess of luck and good fortune, to serve as a memorial of their deed. The Volscians later returned to Roman territory with the Aequians, but the Aequians refused to have Attius Tullius as their leader. This led to a dispute and a fierce battle, in which the Roman people defeated both enemy armies.

487 BC — Minor Battles

Titus Sicinius and Gaius Aquilius were consuls. Sicinius was assigned the province of the Volscians, and Aquilius that of the Hernicians — they, too, had taken up arms. That year, the Hernicians were defeated, but the conflict with the Volscians ended inconclusively, with neither side gaining the upper hand.

Chapter 9

THE AGRARIAN LAW (486-480 BC)

41. SPURIUS CASSIUS AND Proculus Verginius were next appointed as consuls.

During this year, Rome defeated the Hernici people in battle and a treaty was struck with them, taking two-thirds of their land. Consul Cassius planned to divide half of this land among the Latins allies and the other half among the plebeians. To this, he also wanted to add a significant amount of state-owned land, which he claimed had been appropriated by private individuals. Cassius' plan worried many senators, as they were the ones who had taken possession of those formerly public lands. The senators were also concerned that Cassius' gift would give him too much influence among the people and threaten their freedom. This was the first time an Agrarian Law was suggested in Rome's history, a law that always caused major societal upheaval whenever it was brought up, all the way to present day.

FREE LAND, AT WHAT COST?

On the other hand, Consul Verginius opposed the gift and, by doing so, was supported by the senators. Not all plebeians were against him. Some were offended that a gift of land would be given to Roman allies and not just its citizens. Verginius had warned the plebeians in meetings that Cassius' gift was dangerous and would lead to slavery for those who accepted it, implying that Cassius was trying to become a king. "What other reason is there," Verginius asked, "for including the Latin allies and restoring a third of the land to the Hernici which we, ourselves, took from them? Were they not our enemies a short time ago? The reason is clear: these enemy tribes will have Cassius as their leader instead of Coriolanus." Verginius thus became popular for opposing the Agrarian Law.

Both consuls tried to win the favor of the plebeians. Verginius agreed to distribute the lands, however, the lands would go only to Roman citizens. Cassius, who had lost popularity among his countrymen for trying to win over the allies by giving them land, tried to regain the plebeians' favor by distributing the money received for Sicilian grain sales to the plebeians, but the damage was already done. The plebeians rejected this offer of money as an outright bribe to take royal power.

485 BC — THE PLEBEIANS CHANGE THEIR MIND

All sources agree that after Cassius left office, he was immediately condemned and executed. Some sources say his father was the one who tried him at home, then had him whipped and executed. His son's private property was then consecrated to the goddess Ceres and proceeds were used to erect a statue in her honor that was inscribed "Given by the Family of Cassius". I find it easier to believe what others say, that he was tried for high treason by the quaestors, Caeso Fabius and Lucius Valerius, and was condemned by the people. His house, which stood on the open space in front of the Temple of Tellus, was torn down by public decree. Whether the trial was private or public, he was condemned during the consulship of Servius Cornelius Maluginensis and Quintus Fabius Vibulanus.

42. The plebeians' anger toward Cassius didn't last long. The appeal of the Agrarian Law, especially after its original proposer was gone, began to win over the plebeians. This sentiment was further fueled by the untrustworthy and stingy behavior of the senators. After the Volscians and Aequians were defeated that year, Consul Fabius cheated the soldiers out of their spoils of war by selling everything taken from the enemy and putting all the money in the treasury. The name Fabius became unpopular with the plebeians.

484 BC — "INCENTIVES FOR MISCONDUCT"

Despite this, the Senate managed to get Caeso Fabius Vibulanus elected as consul alongside Lucius Aemilius Mamercus. This further angered the plebeians who responded by causing sedition at home, stirring up a war abroad. This led to a pause in civil disagreements as war took precedence.

The patricians and plebeians came together under the leadership of Consul Aemilius and defeated the Volscians and Aequians who had started fighting again. The enemy suffered more losses during the retreat than in the battle, as they were relentlessly chased by the cavalry.

In the same year, the Temple of Castor was dedicated on the fifteenth of July. It had been promised during the war against the Latins under the dictatorship of Posthumius. His son was elected duumvir just so that he could dedicate it.

That year, the plebeians returned back to the Agrarian Law. The plebeian tribunes aimed to increase their power by promoting this popular law. The senators, believing that the people were already too unruly without further provocation, were horrified by the idea of any handouts or incentives for misconduct. The senators found strong allies in the consuls in opposing this and, as a result, they were successful.

483 BC — Empty Promises

They managed to get Marcus Fabius Vibulanus, Caeso's brother, elected as consul for the next year, as well as Lucius Valerius Potitus. Lucius Valerius was especially disliked by the plebeians for his persecution of Spurius Cassius for proposing the Agrarian Law.

That year also saw a struggle with the tribunes. The Agrarian Law was turning out to be something that could not be delivered and its supporters and sponsors were seen as mere braggarts for offering many empty promises that could never be kept. The Fabius name started to gain respect after three consecutive consulships, all of which were marked by resistance with the tribunes. As a result, the office stayed in the Fabius family for a long time.

A war with the Veiians then began, and the Volscians also started fighting again. However, while their strength was more than enough to fight Rome, they misused it by fighting among themselves.

To the public's already troubled state of mind, omens from the heavens were added, showing almost daily threats in the City and the countryside. Seers, consulted by the state and private individuals, sometimes through examining the entrails of animals, sometimes through watching the movement of birds, declared that the only reason for the divine anger was that religious ceremonies weren't being properly observed. These bad omens ended when Oppia, a Vestal Virgin, was found guilty of breaking her vow of chastity and was punished.

482 BC — Escalation

43. Quintus Fabius Vibulanus and Caius Julius Iullus were next appointed as consuls.

This year was marked by ongoing internal strife while foreign wars escalated. The Aequians took up arms and the Veiians began carrying out raids on Roman territory.

481 BC — Military Good Order Breaks

As the concern over these foreign wars grew, they appointed Caeso Fabius Vibulanus, for the second time, and Spurius Furius Fusus as consuls.

The Aequians were besieging Ortona, a Latin city, and the Veiians, having plundered enough, threatened to lay siege to Rome itself. These threats only increased the tension among the plebeians. However, the practice of refusing military service was becoming more common, not by choice, but because Spurius Licinius, a tribune, believed it was time to force the Agrarian Law on the patricians. He took it upon himself to obstruct military preparations. However, he brought resentment upon himself as his tribune colleagues broke with him and joined the consuls in helping them raise an army. Two armies were drafted for the two wars. One was led by Consul Fabius against the Aequians, and the other by Consul Furius against the Veiians. The war against the Veiians didn't yield any significant results.

Fabius, on the other hand, had more trouble with his own people than with the enemy. Despite his military skills and successful strategies, his infantry refused to follow his orders. Even when faced with their own disgrace and potential danger, they refused to speed up their pace or maintain their battle formation, returning to camp in a state of defeat and blaming their general and the cavalry. Consul Fabius, unable to repair the relationship with his men, returned to Rome. His military reputation hadn't improved so much as he had aggravated and embittered the hatred of his soldiers towards him.

480 BC — MANIPULATING WITH KINDNESS

Despite this, the patricians kept the consulship within the Fabius family. They elected Marcus Fabius Vibulanus as consul for the second time and assigned Cnaeus Manlius Cincinnatus as his colleague.

44. In this year, a plebeian tribune named Tiberius Pontificius proposed an Agrarian Law.

He also did what Spurius Licinius had done before: he managed to delay the military draft for a short period. The patricians were once again confused, but Appius Claudius argued that the tribunes' power had been reduced during the previous year, not increased. It was reduced in the present and it would be reduced forever, since there was a way to use the tribunes against each other. He argued that there would always be at least one tribune who would want to gain a personal victory over the others and would want to gain favor with the more influential party by promoting the public good. Multiple tribunes would be ready to support the consuls, if needed, but even just one could be enough to counter all the others.

The solution, he said, was kindness. He urged the consuls and leading senators to win over some of the tribunes to the side of the City and the Senate. The senators and the entire assembly, persuaded by this advice, began treating the tribunes with respect and courtesy, kindly making their appeal for what was beneficial to the state.

Former consuls, by using their personal influence, were able to sway some of the tribunes. Then, with the help of four plebeian tribunes against the one, whom they claimed was obstructing the public good, the consuls were able to complete the draft of men for the army.

Chapter 10

THE ETRUSCANS SENSE WEAKNESS (480 BC)

THE ARMY THEN WENT to war against Veii. Encouragement for the war came from all the Etruscans, but not out of concern for Veiians because they were also Etruscan. Instead, they hoped that Rome would be torn apart by the conflict. In the councils of all the Etruscan states, the leaders openly complained that Rome's power would last forever unless they were torn apart by internal strife. This was the one poison, the one cancer for wealthy states, which made great empires mortal.

THE CANCER OF INDISCIPLINE

This sickness had been endured for a long time partly through the leadership of the senators and partly through the patience of the plebeians. Now, it had come to a breaking point. Two cities had been made from one, with each party having its own magistrates and its own laws. While the Romans had always been rebellious during the draft to gather soldiers for war, once drafted, they had always obeyed their commanders. Regardless of what was happening inside the City, if discipline could be maintained, Rome could withstand any conflict. However, something different was happening now. Roman soldiers were disobeying their superiors, even in the field.

In their latest war, when the army was ready for battle, at the very instant of conflict, they handed over the victory to the conquered Aequians. The Romans deserted their standards, left their general on the field, and had returned, against his orders, to camp. The Etruscans knew, if they persisted, that they could defeat Rome by using its own soldiers against them. All they needed to do was declare war; they believed that fate and the gods would take care of the rest. This hope led the Veiians, who had experienced many ups and downs fighting against Rome, to take up arms.

45. At this point, the Roman consuls were afraid of nothing but their own forces and their own weapons. They remembered the disastrous results of the last war and didn't want to risk facing two armies at once. So, they kept everyone in camp, hoping that time would allow the soldiers to simmer and come to their senses.

Aware of this, the Veii and other Etruscans were aggressive in trying to get them to act. They taunted the Romans first by riding up to the camp and challenging them to fight. When this didn't receive any response, they resorted to yelling insults that the consuls were using the internal conflict as an easy excuse for being cowards. The consuls did believe their soldiers could fight, but didn't trust that they would fight to win. This was a new kind of mutiny, that fully armed men would be both silent and idle. There were also insults hurled about the Romans' heritage, mixing truth with lies. They shouted all these things close to the ramparts and gates of the camp so that everyone would hear. However, despite the insults, the consuls remained patient.

STRATEGIC IDLENESS

The soldiers were affected by it, however, torn between anger and shame. They were distracted from their internal issues and wanted to punish the enemy. But they also didn't want the consuls or the patricians to claim the victory. They were torn between their hatred for the enemy and their resentment towards their leaders.

Eventually, their anger toward the enemy won out. They gathered at the consuls' tent, the *praetorium*, demanding to fight and requesting that the signal should be given. The consuls pretended to consider their request, taking time to talk among themselves. They wanted to fight. However, they decided to suppress this desire and continue to delay, hoping to sharpen the soldiers' eagerness to win. An edict was issued that it wasn't yet time to fight and all soldiers must stay in camp. Anyone who fought without orders would be executed as an enemy. This only made the soldiers even more eager to fight.

The enemy became more aggressive when they heard that the consuls had decided not to fight, knowing that they could now insult the Romans without consequences. "You people can't even be trusted with weapons!" "You can't turn back! It's inevitable!" "Rome has lost!" They hurled insults at the Romans at a fever pitch now, stopping short of storming the camp.

The Roman soldiers could not tolerate this any longer. The entire camp rushed from all sides to the praetorium. This time they didn't make their demands gradually, as before, through the centurions' leaders. Instead, they shouted together from everywhere. The time was right; yet why were the consuls hesitating?

Fabius, realizing his colleague was beginning to concede for fear of a riot, commanded silence with a trumpet blast, and said: "I know that these men, Cnaeus Manlius, can be victorious. However, they've shown that they don't wish to be. Therefore, it is decreed that no signal will be given unless they swear to the gods to return victorious from this battle. Once, in a battle, the soldiers betrayed a Roman consul; but they'll never betray the gods."

A centurion named Marcus Flavoleius, one of the leaders of the battle, was urging them on. He said, "I'll return victorious from the field, Marcus Fabius," invoking the wrath of Jupiter, Mars Gradivus, and the other angry gods if he should fail to keep his vow. Likewise, the entire army swore the same oath. Once all had sworn, the signal was given; they took up their weapons and went toward the fight yelling at the Etruscans to continue their insults. "You, who were so ready with your tongues, stand up now that we're armed!"

On that day, both among the plebeians and the patricians, there was exceptional valor; the name of Fabius stood out the most. They had hoped to reconcile the hostile feelings of the plebeians through that battle, after so many political struggles.

MAN-TO-MAN, SWORDS IN HAND

46. Battle lines were formed. Neither the Veiians nor the Etruscans retreated back; they strongly hoped that the Romans wouldn't engage in battle with them, just as they hadn't engaged with the Aequians. In fact, given everyone's heightened emotions and the criticalness of the situation, the Romans might even perform worse than before.

However, the outcome was completely different. The Roman soldiers fought with more resolve now than they had ever before, in any other war. This was due to the enemy's provocations outside their camp and the consuls delaying the war. The Etruscans barely had time to organize their ranks as Roman spears were thrown hastily, without aim, by the Romans who then quickly closed in for the fiercest type of fighting: man-to-man, swords in hand.

The Fabian family stood out among the rest, setting an example for their fellow citizens. One of them, Quintus Fabius, who had been consul two years prior, was leading an attack on a group of Veiians when, surrounded by the crowd, he was caught off-guard and stabbed in the chest by an Etruscan. When the sword was pulled out, Fabius fell forward onto his wound. One man may have fallen, but both armies felt the impact of his fall, and the Romans began to retreat.

Then, the consul, Marcus Fabius, jumped over the fallen body, raised his shield, and challenged his soldiers, crying, "Was this your oath, men, that you would run away and return to your camp? Do you then fear the most cowardly enemies more than Jupiter and Mars, by whom you swore? But I, though I have sworn no oath, will either return victorious or I will die fighting here by you, Quintus Fabius!"

Caeso Fabius, the consul of the previous year, told his brother, "Do you think any of your words will persuade them to fight, brother? They have sworn to the gods. Let the gods persuade them. And let's, as men of noble birth who are worthy of the name of Fabius, inspire the courage of our soldiers by fighting rather than by preaching!" The two Fabii then charged to the front with their spears, leading the entire line with them.

BLOCK THE EXITS!

47. While the battle resumed on one side, Consul Manlius jumped into the fight on the other side with equal energy. A similar outcome occurred here; just as the soldiers bravely followed Consul Fabius on one wing, they also followed Consul Manlius on this wing with just as much valor, pushing back the enemy to the point of defeat. However, when Manlius was seriously injured and had to withdraw from the battle, the soldiers retreated, thinking he had been killed.

Consul Fabius saw the men retreating and quickly rode over with a detachment of cavalry, shouting that Manlius was still alive and that he was here to help, having just won a victory by defeating the other wing. Manlius then reappeared to continue the battle. The familiar voices of the two consuls reignited the soldiers' courage.

At the same time, the enemy's line was now weakened, but, confident in their larger numbers, they detached their reserve and sent them to attack the Romans' camp. This attack was met with little resistance and so the enemy frittered away their time, their thoughts focused more on looting than fighting. The Roman *triarii*, the oldest soldiers, who had been guarding the camp but hadn't been able to withstand the enemy's first incursion, sent messengers to the consuls telling them the current situation. The triarii then joined together and went to defend the consuls' headquarters without waiting for orders.

Consul Manlius returned to the camp at once and stationed soldiers at all the gates, effectively blocking all possible escape routes. This situation sparked the Etruscans' rage than boldness. They attacked wherever hope showed them an exit, all in vain, until finally a group of young Etruscan soldiers attacked Consul Manlius, easily identifiable by his armor. The first attacks were blocked by those surrounding him, but, eventually, they could not hold off the onslaught. Manlius was fatally wounded and fell, causing those around him to scatter.

The Etruscans then became even more reckless, sending fear through the Romans who were driven through the camp in a panic. The situation would have become dire if not for the lieutenant generals, who quickly grabbed Consul Manlius' body and opened a gate for the enemy to escape. The enemy rushed out from the gate in a chaotic column, and immediately ran into the other victorious consul, Marcus Fabius and his soldiers, where the Etruscans were once again cut to pieces and fled in different directions.

Refusing Glory Makes it Brighter

This was a significant victory, but it was marred by the deaths of Quintus Fabius and Consul Manlius. Consul Fabius, despite being offered a triumph by the Senate, declined. He said that if the army could triumph without their general, he would readily agree to a triumph in recognition of their exceptional performance in the war. However, with his family mourning the death of his brother Quintus Fabius, and the City grieving the loss of one of its consuls, he wouldn't accept the laurel tarnished by public and private sorrow.

The triumph he declined was more notable than any triumph he could have accepted, proving that sometimes, refusing glory at the right time can make it shine even brighter. He then held two funerals for his colleague and brother, delivering the eulogies for both, and by attributing his own merits to them, he himself received the most praise.

Remembering his initial goal as consul, to regain the people's affection, he assigned the injured soldiers to the patricians for treatment. Most of them were given to the Fabii, who took better care of them than anyone else. From then on, the Fabii became popular, not through any schemes, but through their beneficial actions for the state.

Chapter 11

THE FABII BROTHERS
(479-478 BC)

48. THE RESULT WAS that Caeso Fabius was elected consul along-side Titus Verginius. Caeso's election was supported by both the patricians and the plebeians. Instead of focusing on wars or recruitment, he aimed to unite the plebeians and the patricians.

479 BC — CAESO FABIUS

At the start of his term, Caeso suggested that before any tribune — or anyone, for that matter — could advocate an Agrarian Law, the patricians should anticipate it ahead of time and make their own project to review the land taken from the enemy in the recent battle and consider distributing it among the plebeians as fairly as possible. He believed that those who fought for the land should own it. However, the patricians rejected his proposal. Some even criticized Consul Fabius himself, claiming he was becoming care-less and weak due to the excessive glory he had won.

After this, there were no other political struggles in the City.

The Latins were troubled by constant raids by the Aequians. Consul Fabius was sent with an army into Aequian territory to destroy their land. The Aequians reacted by retreating into their towns and staying within their walls, so no significant battle took place.

Consul Verginius' overconfidence led to a defeat from the Veiian enemy. The army would have been completely destroyed if Consul Fabius hadn't arrived in time to help. From then on, there was neither peace nor war with the Veiians, and they acted like thieves. They would run from the Roman troops into their own city, then plunder the countryside when the troops left. This continuous loop of evasion and attack meant that the conflict could neither be resolved or ignored.

Other wars were also looming and imminent, such with the Aequians and Volscians, who seemed to only wait for the pain of their most recent defeat to fade. There were also other future conflicts, such as with the ever-hostile Sabines and all the Etruscans.

A CONSUL AND HIS FAMILY VOLUNTEER

The Veiians had also now become a persistent foe, rather than a dangerous one, who created more irritation to the Romans than alarm. It was never safe for the Romans to neglect the Veiians or to turn their attention elsewhere. The Fabian family went before the Senate about this issue. Consul Fabius, speaking on behalf of the entire family, addressed the senators:

"Fathers, what we need for this war with Veii is a small, constant force, not a large one. If you'll focus on the other wars, we, the Fabii, will take on the responsibility of dealing with the Veiians. We guarantee that the dignity of the Roman name will be safeguarded in that region. We intend to treat this conflict as a personal matter for our family, covering the costs ourselves. The state won't need to provide men or money for us."

The Senate thanked them warmly. The consul, accompanied by other members of the Fabii who had been waiting for the Senate's decision by the entrance, left the Senate for home. They were then ordered to report to the consul's house the next day, armed and ready. After this, they all went home.

49. The news quickly spread throughout the entire City. The Fabii family was praised to the heavens for their taking on the responsibility of the state and making the war with the Veiians their personal battle. If there were two families as strong as the Fabii in the City, they could each take on the Volscians and the Aequians, and all neighboring states could be defeated while the Roman people enjoyed peace.

The next day, the Fabii family prepared for battle. Consul Caeso, dressed in his military cloak, saw his entire family ready to march. He joined them in the center and ordered the standards to be carried forward. Never did an army pass through the City smaller in number but greater in reputation and admiration by the people. All three hundred and six soldiers were patricians from the same family, none of whom anyone would despise as a leader, a senate in their own right in any era. They marched, threatening the Veii with destruction through the power of a single family.

A crowd followed them, made up of their relatives and friends, as well as others who were concerned for the public good. They all admired the Fabii and wished them success, hoping that the Fabii would return with victories that matched their courage and be rewarded with consulships and triumphs.

As they passed the Capitoline Hill, the Citadel, and other sacred buildings, they prayed to whatever gods met their eyes and thoughts for success and a safe return. But these prayers would prove to be in vain. They set up in on ill-fated path, leaving the City through the right portal of the Carmental Gate and arriving at the Cremera River, where they set up a defensive outpost.

478 BC — THREE HUNDRED AND SIX, AND ONE

Lucius Aemilius and Caius Servilius were then elected as consuls.

The Fabii were able to protect their garrison and their own territories as long as the situation involved nothing but raiding by the Veii. They were able to keep their own lands safe and keep the enemy's lands in peril, roaming across the border.

However, this situation changed when the Veiians brought in an Etruscan army and attacked their outpost at the Cremera River. Then Roman troops, led by Consul Aemilius, arrived and fought the Etruscans in a close battle. The Veiians became disorganized and unable to keep their line intact. A wing of the Roman cavalry suddenly came in from the side and ended the battle with the Veii, driving them back to Saxa Rubra, [named for the red rocks nearby], where they had their camp. There, they begged for peace. However, due to the Veiians' fickle character, they soon changed their mind once the Roman garrison had been withdrawn from the Cremera River.

50. The Veiian state once again found itself in conflict with the Fabii family, despite having no additional military resources. This wasn't only a series of minor skirmishes or surprise attacks, but full-scale battles fought in open fields. Remarkably, this single Roman family often emerged victorious over the entire Veiian state, which was one of the most powerful of its time.

Initially, the idea of a single family defeating their army was a source of embarrassment and humiliation for the Veiians. However, they eventually devised a plan to ambush their bold adversaries, taking advantage of the Fabii's growing overconfidence due to their repeated successes. The Veiians began to deliberately leave cattle in the fields seemingly unguarded, and the country people, fleeing, would leave their homes and fields unguarded in a fake retreat. Then, armed Veiians, sent to ward off the raids, feigned fear and ran away. This enticed the Fabii deeper into their territory and further lured them into a false sense of security.

The Fabii's contempt for their enemy grew to the point where they eventually believed they could not be defeated, regardless of the circumstances. It was this overconfidence that led them into the Veiians' trap. They spotted some cattle in the distance from Cremera and rushed towards them, despite the fact that there were a few enemy forces visible. As they ran toward the cattle, the Veiian soldiers waited, hiding on either side of the road. As the Fabii finally scattered to round up the frightened cattle, the trap was sprung trap and enemies stood up, surrounded the Fabii on all sides.

Initially, the Fabii were terrified by the sudden shouting. Then, missiles began to rain down from all sides as the Etruscans, now encircled by armed men, pushed toward them. The Fabii now formed into a defensive, tight circle. However, this only highlighted their small numbers as compared to the Etruscans because they were so densely packed together.

Abandoning the circle strategy, the Fabii then focused all their efforts on breaking through the line by using their bodies and weapons in a wedge formation. They eventually forced their way through the line of soldiers and to a nearby hill. Once they reached the higher ground, they were able to catch their breath and regain their composure. They managed to hold off the advancing Veiians, and it seemed they might even win, thanks to their advantageous position. However, a Veiian detachment who had been sent around the ridge emerged upon the top of the hill, thus giving the enemy the advantage once again.

In the end, all the Fabii were killed, and their outpost was captured. It is universally agreed that all three hundred and six Fabii were killed in the battle and only one, a boy on the cusp of manhood, Quintus

Fabius, survived to continue the Fabian line. He would later prove to be a crucial asset to the Roman people in times of both domestic and military crisis.

Chapter 12

Consulship Is a Death Sentence (477-473 BC)

51. WHEN THE NEWS of the Fabii disaster reached Rome, Caius Horatius and Titus Menenius were serving as consuls.

Menenius was quickly dispatched to confront the Etruscans, still joyous from their victory. Yet again, a battle ensued in which the Romans performed poorly, and the enemy then took control of the Janiculum Hill.

The City would have been besieged, with food supplies dwindling due to the war and the Etruscans crossing the Tiber, had it not been for Consul Horatius being recalled from the war with the Volscians. The war was so close to the City that the first battle took place near the Temple of Hope, with uncertain results, and a second one at the Colline Gate. Here, the Romans had a slight advantage, but the victory boosted the soldiers' morale for future battles.

476 BC — USING CATTLE AS BAIT (AGAIN)

Aulus Verginius and Spurius Servilius were then elected as consuls.

After their defeat in the last battle, the Veiians decided against outright confrontation in the form of war. Instead, they resorted to raiding Roman territory, treating the Janiculum Hill as their own private fortress. Neither the livestock nor the farmers were safe. However, the Romans used a trap against them similar to the one they, themselves, had used against the Fabii. They deliberately chased some cattle out to bait the Veiians, who then tried to capture them and thus fell into an ambush by the Romans. As the Veiians' numbers were greater, the slaughter was greater.

This disaster fueled a bitter rage by the Veiians, ultimately leading to an even bigger disaster. They crossed the Tiber at night and tried to attack Consul Servilius' camp. Driven back by heavy losses, they barely managed to make it back to the Janiculum Hill. Consul Servilius, in response, then followed them, crossing the Tiber, and setting up his camp at the foot of the Janiculum Hill.

The next morning, motivated by the previous day's successes (more likely, they were driven by the shortage of food), Servilius led his army up to the enemy camp at the top of the Janiculum. Driven back more disgracefully than the day before, the Consul and his army were saved by the timely arrival of his colleague, Consul Verginius. Then, the Etruscans, trapped between the two armies, were completely wiped out. Thus, a risky move by the Romans ended the Veiian war successfully.

RETURN OF PEACE, FOOD, AND IDLENESS

52. With the return of peace, the City saw an increase in grain. Grain was brought in from Campania and, as fears of future famine subsided, the grain that had been hoarded was released. With abundance, plenty of time for leisure, and no external threats to complain about, the plebeians searched for problems at home. The tribunes, as usual, began to stir them up with their poison, pushing for an Agrarian Law and inciting them against any patricians who opposed it.

This opposition wasn't just against the senators as a whole, but also against specific people. Quintus Considius and Titus Genucius, the proponents of the Agrarian Law, set a trial date for Titus Menenius, charging him with the loss of the garrison at the Cremera Fort. This attack had occurred while he was consul and, despite his camp not being far away, he didn't offer assistance. Despite the senators' efforts to defend him and the lingering popularity of his father Agrippa, Menenius was personally devastated by the charges. The plebeian tribunes, however, didn't seek the death penalty. The imposed a fine of two-thousand pounds of *aes rude*, or rough bronze nuggets, on him, even though they had accused him of a capital offense. The penalty affected him deeply. It's said that he could not bear the disgrace and mental anguish, and that he died by illness as a result.

Soon after, the former consul, Spurius Servilius, was indicted by the tribunes Lucius Caedicius and Titus Statius, just as he left office. Unlike Menenius, Servilius didn't plead for mercy from the tribunes but instead faced them with total confidence in his innocence and his popularity. He was charged with the battle against the Etruscans at the Janiculum. However, he was just as bold defending himself as he was with defending the state. In a fiery speech, he reprimanded both the tribunes and the plebeians, then condemned them for the trial and death of Titus Menenius, whose father had previously helped the plebeians regain the very rights that they now enjoyed. His colleague Verginius was brought forward as a witness to support him, however, it was the condemnation of Menenius that helped him the most, as popular opinion on the matter had changed.

475 BC — LATIN ALLIES OVERSTEP RULES

53. [Publius Valerius (Publicola) and Caius Nautius were then elected as consuls. — lcw.]

The domestic disputes had been resolved, but a new war with Veii had begun in which the Sabines had joined their forces. Consul Publicola, after calling for reinforcements from the Latins and Hernicians, was sent to Veii with an army. He immediately attacked the Sabine camp, located outside the walls of Veii. This caused such a panic that the Sabines scattered in different directions to fend off the attack and the gate through which the Romans advanced was captured.

Inside the camp, it was more of a massacre than a battle. The pandemonium spread into the city of Veii, leaving to the Veiians rushing to arms in a panic as if Veii had been captured. Some went to support the Sabines, while others attacked the Romans, who had focused all their effort on the Sabine camp. For a short time, the Romans were disoriented and confused as they were attacked on two sides. Then they, too, formed two fronts with their standards turned in both directions, and held their ground. Consul Publicola ordered the cavalry to charge, which defeated the Etruscans and sent them fleeing. In the same hour, two armies and two of the most powerful neighboring states were defeated.

While these events were happening at Veii, the Volscians and Aequians had set up their camp in the territory of Latin allies and were ravaging the land. The Latins, with the help of the Hernicians and without any Roman generals or Roman reinforcements, drove them out of their camp. In addition to recovering their own possessions, they gained a lot of spoils. However, Consul Nautius was sent from Rome to join the Latins and Hernicians to fight the Volscians.

It was, I believe, not acceptable for allies to wage wars with their own forces and under their own command without a Roman general and troops. The Volscians were subjected to all kinds of abuse and humiliation, but they still refused to engage in a field battle.

474 BC — TEMPORARY PEACE

54. Lucius Furius and Caius Manlius Vulso were the next to become consuls.

Manlius was given command of the forces against the Veiians. However, there was no war with them. Instead, a forty-year truce was agreed upon at the Veiians' request such that, instead of fighting, they were required to provide grain and pay tribute.

Immediately following peace abroad, there was more unrest at home as the tribunes agitated for an Agrarian Law and goaded the plebeians into a frenzy. The consuls, neither scared by Menenius' condemnation nor the danger faced by Servilius, fought back strongly. Cnaeus Genucius, a tribune, seized and impeached the consuls when they left office.

473 BC — FASCES IS A FUNERAL DECORATION

Lucius Aemilius Mamercus for the third time and Opiter Verginius became the new consuls. In some records, instead of Verginius, Vopiscus Julius Iullus is listed as consul.

Whomever the consuls were, in this year the consuls from the previous year, Lucius Furius and Caius Manlius, were called to trial before the people. They had been dressed as if they were mourning and were appealing not just to the plebeians but also to younger senators with a warning: stay away from honors and the administration of public affairs. The symbols of power: the consular fasces, the *praetexta*, and the *curule chair* were nothing more than funeral decorations, they said.

Those who wore a distinguished symbol like the white woolen toga were actually wearing sacrificial garlands and they were destined for death.

For those who still wanted to be consul, they said, those people should know that the consul's power was controlled and suppressed by the tribunes and the consul had to obey the tribunes' orders as if he were a servant. If the consul sided with the patricians or thought there were any other group in the state besides the plebeians, he should remember the exile of Coriolanus and the humiliation and eventual death of Titus Menenius.

These speeches stirred up the senators. From then on, they held their meetings in private, away from the general public. They agreed that they had to save the accused, whether lawful or not. The most violent proposals were the most popular. They were ready to do anything, no matter how bold.

Upon the day of the trial, the plebeians waited in the Forum. They were surprised when the tribune who originally impeached the consuls, Cnaeus Genucius, didn't appear. Was he was being intimidated by the patricians? Was the people's cause being abandoned? Finally, news came that the tribune had been found dead in his house. This news caused panic and, just as an army breaks up when its commander is killed, everyone scattered in all directions. The other tribunes were scared, realizing that the Sacred Laws offered them little protection.

However, the patricians were overjoyed. They were so far from regretting the crime they committed that even those who were innocent were trying to appear as though they had a key part in it. They openly declared that the power of the tribunes should be beaten into submission.

Chapter 13

APPIUS CLAUDIUS AND VOLERO (473-471 BC)

55. RIGHT AFTER THIS win, which set a dangerous precedent, a new draft for soldiers was announced. With the tribunes now intimidated, the consuls were able to carry out their plan without any resistance. The plebeians were now angrier about the tribunes being silent and less angry about the consuls giving orders. Their freedom was over and that they were back to the old ways. The power of the tribunes, they said, had died with Tribune Genucius and was now buried with him. A new idea was needed to resist the senators.

They believed that the only solution was for the plebeians to defend themselves, since nobody else was defending them. The consuls had twenty-four *lictors*, or bodyguards, who were from the plebeians. These men were the most contemptible and weakest of all. They could be easily defeated, if only the plebeians would stand up to them.

A CENTURION SPARKS CHANGE

After talking about these issues, they turned to Volero Publilius, a plebeian and former centurion now opposed to the draft and being made a common soldier. The consuls sent a lictor to arrest him. He appealed to the tribunes, but none came to his aid. The consuls then ordered Volero to be stripped and the rods prepared for punishment. "I appeal to the people," Volero said, "since the plebeian tribunes would rather see a Roman citizen whipped before their eyes than themselves be murdered in their beds by you." The more emphatically he shouted, the more violently the lictor tried to tear off his toga and strip him.

Then Volero, a man of exceptional strength, pushed the lictor off with the help of the crowd. Amidst the indignant yelling of his supporters at his treatment, he retreated into the thickest part of the crowd, crying out, "I appeal to the plebeians for your support! Stand by me, fellow citizens! Stand by me, fellow soldiers! Don't expect any help from the tribunes. They need your help just like I do!"

The people were stirred up as if for battle, and it was clear that a critical confrontation would be imminent. There was a real danger that people wouldn't respect any rules or rights. The consuls tried to face the situation but quickly found that there was little safety for authority without strength. The lictors were then mobbed, the fasces were broken, and the consuls were driven from the Forum into the Senate, uncertain how far Volero would push his victory.

Once the disturbance had calmed down, the consuls called a meeting of the Senate and complained about the outrage they suffered, the violence of the plebeians, and Volero's audacity and insolence. Although some gave violent speeches, the older members advised against reacting to the rashness of the plebeians with anger.

472 BC — VOLERO BECOMES TRIBUNE

56. The plebeians, who strongly supported Volero, elected him as tribune in the next election for the year in which Lucius Pinarius Mamercinus Rufus and Publius Furius Medullinus Fusus served as consuls.

Despite expectations that Volero would use his position to harass the previous year's consuls, he prioritized public interest over his own personal grudges. He didn't criticize the consuls but instead proposed a law that tribunes should be elected at the Comitia Tributa, the tribal assemblies.

The proposal seemed harmless at first, but it actually took away the power of the patricians to elect tribunes of their choice through the votes of their clients, the slaves whom they had freed. The patricians strongly opposed this proposal, though it was very popular among the plebeians. Despite their efforts, the patricians could not convince any of their colleagues to protest against it, which was their only remaining option for the year. The issue carried its own momentum and dragged on throughout the rest of the year without resolution.

471 BC — SHOULD PLEBEIANS ELECT THEIR OWN REPRESENTATIVES?

The plebeians re-elected Volero as a tribune the following year. The senators, anticipating a battle that might escalate into a crisis, elected Appius Claudius Crassus and Titus Quinctius Capitolinus Barbatus as consuls. Even before he had taken office, Appius was disliked by the plebeians due to past conflicts with his father, Appius Claudius Sabinus.

At the start of the year, this new proposed law, the *Lex Publilia,* was the most important issue. Although Volero initiated it, his colleague, Laetorius, was a fresher and fiercer advocate. He enjoyed a great reputation as a soldier and there was no one his age more skilled in combat. While Volero focused on the law and avoided criticizing the consuls, Laetorius accused Appius and his family of being harsh and cruel towards the Roman plebeians. Appius, he said, was elected by the patricians not as a consul, but as a butcher to torment and tear apart the people. However, the infectiousness of Laetorius' enthusiasm didn't match his eloquence, as a man of the military. "I have difficulty speaking my mind to prove what I've said," he told them. "Citizens, be here tomorrow. I'll either die here in your presence or carry through the law."

On the next day, the tribunes took over the speaker's platform in the comitium before anyone else. The consuls and patricians gathered in the assembly to block the law. Laetorius ordered everyone except voters to leave, but the young patricians ignored him and refused to go, so he ordered them to be arrested. Consul Appius declared that a tribune had no authority over anyone except a plebeian. Laetorius could not even remove them by force, according to ancestral custom. All he was allowed to say was "If it pleases you, citizens, depart." Appius then confused Laetorius by derisively debating the legalities.

Laetorius, enraged, sent his officer to Consul Appius, who responded by sending his own lictor back to the tribune, shouting at him that he was a private citizen who had no authority or office. Laetorius would have been roughly treated except the assembly jumped up, angrily, to defend the tribune against the consul. As this was happening, people flooded in from the street to see what was happening. Despite the mounting tension, Appius Claudius stood firm.

The situation would have escalated further bloodshed if not for the intervention of Consul Quinctius, who ordered the senators who had been prior consuls to remove Laetorius with force, if necessary. Quinctius then tried to calm the angry plebeians with prayers and asked the tribunes to dismiss the assembly, assuring them that a delay wouldn't diminish their power but would add wisdom to their strength. He also promised that the senators would be under the control of the plebeians, and the consul under the power of the senators.

No Unity When All Seek Everything

57. While Consul Quinctius struggled to calm down the people, the senators had an even harder time calming down the other consul, Appius Claudius. After the plebeian assembly was finally dismissed, the consuls called a meeting of the Senate. There, despite the varying opinions fluctuating between fear and anger, as time passed, the senators became less inclined to continue the conflict after they had been given a chance to think. They gave their thanks to Consul Quinctius for his efforts in calming the situation.

They asked Appius Claudius to agree that the power of the consul should only be as great as it could be while still maintaining a peaceful state. If the plebeian tribunes were pulling all of the power toward themselves while the consuls were pulling all power to themselves, there was no strength left in the middle; no basis for common action. There was too much concern about who would rule the troubled and divided State, rather than on why it was troubled and divided in the first place.

Consul Appius, however, called on gods and men to witness that Rome was being betrayed and abandoned due to cowardice. It wasn't the consuls who were failing the Senate, but the Senate was failing the consuls. He argued that they were now accepting laws that were more oppressive than those approved on the Sacred Mount. However, defeated by the unanimous opinion of the senators, he gave in and the law, Lex Publilia, was passed without any opposition.

FIRST TRIBUNES ELECTED IN THE ASSEMBLY

58. For the first time, tribes elected the tribunes in the *Comitia Tributa*. Piso stated that three were added to the existing two. The plebeian tribunes were named Cnaeus Siccius, Lucius Numitorius, Marcus Duilius, Spurius Icilius, and Lucius Mecilius.

During the period of unrest in Rome, a war with the Volscians and Aequians began. They had entered the Roman land laying waste wherever they went, providing a potential refuge for plebeians who might want to secede and join them. As the internal disputes were resolved, they retreated to their camps and moved them further away. Appius Claudius was dispatched to confront the Volscians, while Quinctius was assigned the Aequians as his province

Appius Claudius was as harsh in war as he was at home, his severity unchecked due to his freedom from interference by the tribunes. He harbored a deep resentment for the plebeians, much more so than his father. They had defeated him and, when he was appointed as the one consul who could counter the tribunes' influence, the Lex Publilia was passed during his consulate. This was a law that previous consuls, obstructed much less than he was, were able to block.

ENEMY FINDS ROMAN CRUELTY WEAK

His anger and indignation stirred his domineering spirit to torment the army. However, the soldiers could not be subdued. They carried out every order slowly, lazily, carelessly, and defiantly. Neither shame nor fear held them back. If he wanted the army to move quickly, they deliberately disobeyed and moved slower. If he tried to motivate them, they would reduce their efforts. When he was present, they would lower their eyes, but as he passed by they would curse him.

Despite his outward indifference to plebeian hatred, he was still sometimes affected by it. After all attempts failed trying to accomplish anything with such harsh treatment, he stopped interacting with the soldiers. He claimed the army was corrupted by the centurions and mocked the centurions as "Volerones" with sarcasm.

59. The Volscians were aware of the situation and pushed forward with increased energy. They hoped that the Roman army would resist Consul Appius just as they had resisted Consul Fabius in the past. In truth, the Roman army's hostility towards Appius was even stronger than it had been toward Fabius. Unlike Fabius' army who merely refused to win, the current army actively wanted to lose. When they were led to the battlefield, they retreated to their camp in a shameful flight. They only stood their ground when they saw the Volscians approaching their fortifications and slaughtering the rear of their army. At that point, they fought to prevent the nearly victorious enemy from breaching their lines. It was clear that the Roman soldiers didn't want their camp to be captured, but in all other areas they took pride in their defeat and humiliation.

Despite these circumstances, Appius remained resolute and wanted to intensify his cruelty. When he called an assembly, the lieutenant generals and military tribunes gathered around him warned not to try to see how far he could stretch his authority, for his authority wholly depended upon the free consent of those who obeyed it. The soldiers refused to attend the assembly and their complaints could be heard everywhere, demanding that the camp be moved away from Volscian territory. The generals warned him that the enemy had recently been at their gates and ramparts, and that there weren't only suspicions of a serious mutiny, but the evidence was now right before their eyes. Eventually, Appius gave in, realizing that they were gaining nothing but a delay in their punishment. He dismissed the assembly and gave orders were issued for a march the next morning.

At dawn, the trumpet gave the signal for the march. As the column moved out the camp, the Volscians, as if they were alerted by the same signal, attacked the Romans from the rear. The panic spread to the front, causing such confusion that standards and formations were disrupted, commands could not be heard, and lines could not be formed. Everyone was focused on escaping.

In chaos, the soldiers scattered, jumping over piles of dead bodies and discarded weapons. They only escaped because the Volscians eventually stopped pursuing them before the Romans stopped running.

ONE SIDE, DECIMATION

After Appius Claudius had tried, in vain, to rally his men, the scattered troops gradually came together again. The consul ordered the camp to be placed inside peaceful territory which had been undisturbed by war. After this was done, he then called up the men for an assembly.

At the convened assembly, he chastised the army as traitors for their betrayal of military discipline and desertion of their standards. He then demanded to know from each soldier, individually, where his missing standard was or where his missing weapon was. Every unarmed soldier who had thrown away his weapon, every standard bearer who had lost his standard, every centurion or *duplarius*, a low-level officer, who had deserted his rank, was identified. All were ordered to be beaten with rods and then executed by beheading.

As for the rest of the soldiers, every tenth soldiers was selected, by lot, and then executed.

OTHER SIDE, RESPECT

60. On the other hand, Consul Quinctius and the Roman soldiers in the Aequian territory competed in showing courtesy and kindness. Quinctius was naturally gentler, and the harshness of his colleague led him to take greater pleasure in expressing his good nature more.

The Aequians didn't dare to confront this strong bond between a general and his army. Instead, they allowed the enemy to roam their lands without resistance to seek out plunder, resulting in the largest collection of spoils of any previous war. All the spoils which went to the soldiers. They also received praise, which they enjoyed as much as rewards. The army returned with a better opinion of their general and the patricians, saying that they had a father in their general, whereas the other army had a tyrant.

The year, marked by mixed success in war and intense conflicts at home and abroad, was most notable for the tribal assembly elections. The significance of the victory was more symbolic than practical. The exclusion of the patricians from the elections diminished their dignity more than any actual shift in power between the plebeians or patricians.

Chapter 14

RETURN TO THE AGRARIAN LAW (470-468 BC)

61. A MORE TURBULENT year followed, with Lucius Valerius Potitus and Tiberius Aemilius Mamercus serving as consuls, because of the ongoing disputes over the Agrarian Law and the trial of Appius Claudius.

Appius Claudius was such a strong opponent of the law and a supporter of those who owned public land that he began acting like a third consul. As a result, the tribunes, Marcus Duilius and Caius Sicinius, summoned him to trial. This was the first time someone so despised by the plebeians was indicted. Appius Claudius was widely resented not just for his own actions but also for those of his father.

AS INTIMIDATING ON TRIAL AS IN POWER

The patricians put substantially more effort in defending him than they did for others. They saw Appius Claudius as a defender of the Senate and its authority. Yes, they said, he had overstepped the boundaries in his struggle, but he was being unjustly targeted for his aggressive stance. Appius himself was the only patrician who didn't take the tribunes, the plebeians, or even his trial seriously. He refused to change his clothing or humbly grasp hands to beg for mercy. He didn't soften his fiery manner of speaking when he had to defend himself before the people. His facial expression, his stubborn gaze, and his arrogant speech were all the same. Many of the plebeians were as intimidated by Claudius on trial as they had been when he was consul.

He defended himself once, with the same accusatory tone he always used. His fearlessness shocked the tribunes and the plebeians so much that they voluntarily postponed his trial and allowed the matter to be delayed. However, before the rescheduled trial could take place, Claudius died of an illness.

When the tribunes tried to prevent his funeral eulogy, the plebeians disagreed. Such a significant man, they said, shouldn't be denied the customary honors on his last day. They listened to his eulogy as attentively as they had listened to the accusations against him when he was alive, and they attended his funeral in large numbers.

62. In the same year, Consul Valerius led an army against the Aequians. When he was unable to provoke the enemy into a battle, he attempted to raid their camp. However, a severe thunderstorm showered down hail, halting the Romans' attempt. They were even more surprised when, after the retreat had been sounded, a tranquil and cloudless sky returned, as if the camp were defended by divine power. The Consul felt that such a sign meant it would be an act of impiety to attack a second time. Instead, they focused their efforts on destroying the countryside.

Meanwhile, Consul Aemilius was leading a war against the Sabines. Since the enemy stayed within their walls, the Romans destroyed their lands. They burned not only the country houses but also the villages, which were densely populated. This provoked the Sabines, who left their walls to confront the invaders. After a battle that ended without a clear winner, the Sabines moved their camp to a safer location the next day. To the consul, this seemed like a sufficient enough reason to leave the enemy as defeated, even though the war was still unresolved.

469 BC — ONGOING FOREIGN CONFLICTS

63. During these conflicts, while domestic disagreements persisted, Titus Numicius Priscus and Aulus Verginius were chosen as consuls.

The plebeians would no longer tolerate any further postponements of the Agrarian Law. A violent protest was being plotted when it was discovered, through the smoke of burning farms and the fleeing of farmers into the City, that the Volscians were approaching. This situation halted the rebellion, now on the verge of erupting. The consuls, immediately pushed into war by the Senate, led the young men out of the City, and this calmed the rest of the plebeians. The enemy, having done nothing more than scare the Romans with baseless fear, marched away quickly in retreat.

Consul Numicius went to Antium to fight the Volscians, while Consul Verginius fought against the Aequians. With the Aequians, a significant defeat was narrowly avoided due to an ambush, but the courage of the soldiers restored the Roman dominance which had been jeopardized by the consul's negligence. Matters were handled better against the Volscians. The enemy was defeated in the first battle and forced to retreat into the city of Antium, a very affluent and prosperous place in those times. The consul, not daring to attack Antium, seized another town, Caeno, from the people of Antium, which wasn't as affluent.

While the Aequians and Volscians occupied the Roman armies, the Sabines plundered the Roman lands all the way to the City gates. A few days later, however, the Sabines suffered more destruction than they had inflicted as the two consuls angrily entered the Sabine terri-tories and destroyed it.

468 BC — Starting in War, Ending in Peace

64. Toward the end of the year, there was a brief period of peace. However, as usual, it was disrupted by conflicts between the patricians and the plebeians. The plebeians, out of frustration, refused to par-ticipate in the consular elections this year. As a result, Titus Quinctius and Quintus Servilius were elected consuls by the patricians and their clients.

Their year in office was similar to the previous one, starting with turmoil and ending with peace due to an external war. The Sabines, quickly moving across the plains of Crustuminum, caused destruc-tion along the banks of the Anio River. They were pushed back when they reached the Colline Gate and the City walls, but they managed to take a significant amount of people and livestock. Consul Servilius, despite his determined army, was unable to catch up with the main Sabine force. However, he caused so much destruction that he re-turned with more plunder than the Sabines had taken.

In the war against the Volscians, the Romans did well thanks to the efforts of both the consul and the soldiers. They first fought a fierce battle on equal ground with heavy casualties on both sides. The Romans, due to their smaller numbers, would have retreated if the consul hadn't encouraged them by shouting, falsely, that the enemy was retreating on the other wing. As the Romans believed they were winning, they charged and turned the tide of the battle, winning a victory for the Romans.

The consul, fearing that continuing to press too hard might renew the battle, signaled for a retreat. A few days of rest followed, during which a large number of people from all the Volscian and Aequian states came to the enemy camp, believing that the Romans would retreat in the night if they saw them. Around the third watch, they came to attack the Roman camp.

HORNS AND TRUMPETS AS WEAPONS

Consul Quinctius, calming the confusion caused by the sudden alarm, ordered the soldiers to remain quietly in their quarters. He then marched out a cohort of Hernician allies to their outposts. There, he ordered the horn-blowers and trumpeters to mount up on horseback and blow their instruments at full volume all night, to keep the enemy on alert until daylight. Back at camp, the rest of the night was quiet and the Roman soldiers had the advantage of a good night's sleep. On the Volscian side, it was anything but restful. The sight of armed infantry, whom they believed to be greater in number, kept them wide awake and in a perpetual state of readiness, as did the neighing and snorting of horses, aggravated at the loud noise in their ears and unusual weight of their riders.

65. As the day broke, the Romans, rejuvenated and rested from sleep, were led into battle. On the first charge, they quickly overwhelmed the Volscians, who were tired from standing and lack of sleep. However, it was more like a retreat than a rout. The hills behind them provided a safe escape for them, and the ranks behind the front line remained intact. Consul Quinctius, upon reaching the rising hill, stopped the army. Soldiers were shouting, demanding to continue the pursuit of the now-disheartened enemy, but were held back.

The cavalry, gathering around the consul, were even more aggressive, calling out that they would move forward ahead of the standards. The consul was unsure. He trusted his men's bravery but not the terrain. The soldiers cried out that they were moving forward and then acted on their words. They stuck their spears into the ground to make themselves lighter and charged up the steep hill.

The Volscians, having thrown their spears at the first attack, now rolled stones at the advancing Romans, striking them repeatedly from their higher position. This almost defeated the Romans' left wing, and they started to retreat, but Consul Quinctius scolded his retreating men for first being reckless and now being cowardly. These words made their fear give way to a sense of shame.

At first, they held their ground with determination as they re-formed their line. Then, as their strength allowed, they began to advance against the Volscians. They renewed their battle cry, encouraging the entire army to move forward. With a restored effort, they managed to climb the hill and overcome the steepness of the terrain.

Just as they were about to reach the top of the hill and charge a second time, the enemy turned and fled. Both the pursuers and the pursued flooded into the Volscian camp almost simultaneously. In the ensuing panic, the camp was captured. Those Volscians who could escape headed toward Antium. The Roman army then marched towards Antium and, after a few days of siege, Antium surrendered. This wasn't due to any additional force from the Romans, but because the Volscians' morale had been broken from the unsuccessful battle and the loss of their camp.

DICTIONARY

AEDILE – THE POSITION of aedile was an elected office of the plebeians. Two aediles were responsible for maintenance of public buildings, the running of public festivals, games, and the supply of food in the marketplace. They also were responsible for public order. See Curule Aedile for the position changing.

AES RUDE – Sometimes called "assis, as, asses, or ass". Irregularly shaped pieces of bronze known as aes rude (*rough bronze*) which needed to be weighed for each transaction. The bronze nuggets usually weighed 5 pounds each. As an example: fines or bail at a surety of 3,000 aes rude would be 15,000 pounds. Ten sureties would be 150,000 pounds.

AGRARIAN LAW - (Latin *ager*, meaning "land") There existed two kinds of land in ancient Rome: private and public land (*ager publicus*), which included common pasture. There were various attempts by the plebeians to regulate the laws of public land distribution. This struggle was ongoing for many years between the patricians and the plebeians which was known as the Conflict of Orders.

ANCILIA - (sing. ancile) The original ancile was said to have fallen from the skies in the time of Numa. In order to protect it from damage or robbery, Numa had 11 shields made just like it to disguise the original. The shape of the shield was unusual in that it was shaped like an oval but the sides were indented in a long curve. These twelve shields, "ancilia", were kept in the Temple of Mars Gradivus and on the kalends of March (March 1st) they were taken out to celebrate a feast to Mars Gradivus. The feast lasted several days with the twelve Salii, or priests of Mars, carrying the sacred shields about the city, singing songs in praise of Mars Gradivus, Numa, and Mamurius Veturius, who created the eleven copies. While performing a dance, the twelve Salii sang and they struck the shield with rods, emphasizing the rhythm of the song.

ARUSPEX - (aruspices, sing.) In ancient Rome, a priest who practiced the foretelling of events, especially by examining the internal organs of animals.

ATELLAN FARCE - (aka Oscan Games) Masked impromptu rustic plays of country life and adopted for intermissions and after plays during the Republic and up to the time of Tiberius. The stock characters' masks were generally grotesque.

AUGUR - One of the members of a religious college whose job was to watch for and interpret the activities of birds. These signs (auspices) could be positive or negative and were sent by the gods as a comment on any proposed undertaking. Auspex, another word for augur, can be translated to "one who looks at birds".

AUSPICES - (Latin auspicium) Which means "looking at birds". Depending upon the birds, the auspices from the gods could be positive or negative (auspicious or inauspicious). The augurs job was to read the flights of birds to determine the will of the Gods. The auspices showed the Romans that it may or may not be a good thing they were about to do. There was no explanation for the decision, just that it was the will of the gods.

AUSPEX – See **AUGUR**

BEADLE – A beadle is an official who may usher, keep order, make reports, and assist in religious functions; or a minor official who carries out various civil, educational or ceremonial duties of a household. Beadles also had the responsibility of maintaining discipline during the observance of public worship.

BUCKLER – The buckler was a small shield that usually fit on the wrist or forearm of the soldier and was used by the cavalry or in hand-to-hand combat.

CAESO QUINCTIUS - Caeso Quinctius L. f. L. n. Cincinnatus was the son of the Dictator. During the political struggles between the patricians and the plebeians Caeso took the side of the patricians and, though having no position of power or title, he and his followers prevented the plebeian tribunes and plebeians from meeting in the Forum and conducting their business. They did this by using violence to drive away the plebeians. His trial for obstructing the plebeian tribunes in 461 BC was one of the key events in the Conflict of Orders in the years that led up to the decemvirate.

CENSOR - A censor was one of two senior magistrates in the city of ancient Rome who supervised public morals, maintained the census, and supervised tax obligations. The job was given to former consuls and lasted up to 18 months.

CINCINNATUS - Lucius Quinctius Cincinnatus was a Roman patrician of the Quinctius family who was a statesman and military leader of the early Roman Republic who became a legendary figure of Roman virtue—particularly civic virtue—by the time of the late Republic.

CIRCUMVALLATION - The military process of surrounding an enemy fort with armed forces to prevent entry or escape. It serves both to cut communications with the outside world and to prevent supplies and reinforcements from being introduced.

CITADEL - The citadel was a fortified hill that is often located within a city or town on which several temples were built. Often there was a fortified structure designed to protect the citizens against enemies.

CIVIC CROWN - A wreath of oak leaves woven to form a crown. It was awarded to Roman citizens who saved the life of a fellow citizen being threatened by an enemy usually in or near the City. The citizen saved must attest to it and no one else was a witness.

CLIENT - In Rome a client was a free man who entrusted himself to another and received protection in return. A client was a bonafide position, hereditary, and recognized by law although not defined or enforced. The law was more rigid in the case of the freedman (freed slave), who was automatically a client of his former owner. Ordinary clients supported their patron in political and private life and accompanied him when he went out. The size of a man's group of clients, their wealth and status, added to his prestige, popularity, and political power. In exchange, clients received benefits of various kinds, such as food or money and help in the courts.

COHORT – A legionary cohort of the early republic consisted of six *centuriae*, or centuries, each consisting of 80 legionaries, for a total of 480 men.

COLLEGE OF PONTIFFS - The College of Pontiffs (Collegium Pontificum) were the highest-ranking priests of the state religion. The members of the college were the Pontifex Maximus and the other pontifices, the rex sacrorum, the 15 flamens, and the Vestal Virgins.

COLLEGIUM - A collegium (pl.: collegia) or college was any group in ancient Rome that acted as a legal entity. They could be civil or religious. The word "collegium" literally means "society". They functioned as social clubs or religious groups sharing the same variety of interests such as: politics, religion, different professions, civic duties or trade activities. These associations helped the members' influence on politics and the economy and encouraged them to act as lobbying groups and representatives for traders and merchants.

COMITIA CURIATA - Composed of 30 curiae, or local groups, drawn from three ancient tribes, assembly of these curiae, the Comitia Curiata, was for a time the sole legal representative of the entire Roman people. The Comitia Curiata dates from the time of the Roman kings. During the Republic it was a general assembly but only patricians could vote. It was here that the military tribunes, consuls, consular tribunes, praetors, etc. were elected.

COMITA TRIBUTA - This was an assembly consisting of all Roman plebeians organized by tribes and it excluded patricians. It was convened to make decisions on legislative or judicial matters, or to hold elections. Patricians felt they were not bound by these laws as they were not included. This changed later on.

COMITIUM - The Comitium was the original open-air public meeting space of ancient Rome. The Comitium was in front of the meeting house of the Roman Senate – the Curia Hostilia. It was the meeting place of the Curiate Assembly, the earliest popular assembly of organized voting divisions of the Republic. Later, during the Roman Republic, the Tribal Assembly and the Plebeian Assembly met there.

CONFLICT OF THE ORDERS – also Struggle of the Orders, was a political struggle between the plebeians (commoners) and patricians (aristocrats) of the ancient Roman Republic lasting from 500 BC to 287 BC in which the plebeians sought political equality with the patricians.

CONSUL – A consul was the highest elected public official of the Roman Republic (c. 509 BC to 27 BC). Normally two were elected to lead for one year. The consul was the second highest position in power below that of the censor held by previous consuls.

CONSULARS AND CONSULAR RANK – Former consuls were often called upon to fill in when additional help was needed. Sometimes former consuls were assigned new duties (e.g., guarding Rome while the current consuls were away at battle). The Romans were smart in utilizing former consuls, because these men had the experience and expertise to handle critical jobs. Another former consul role was that of pro consul which was an extension of the consul's year to act as a representative of the new consul, usually in battles and for no more than 6 months.

CONSULAR TRIBUNES – Military tribunes with consular power were created during the Conflict of the Orders, along with the position of the censor, in order to give the plebeian order access to higher levels of government without having to reform the office of consul; plebeians could be elected to the office of consular tribune. The consular tribunes often replaced the consuls as the leaders. The consular tribunes not only handled the military affairs of Rome, but also the administrative needs of the City as well.

CO-OPT - Appointing an individual to membership of a committee or other body by invitation of the existing members. The passage of *Lex Trebonia* forbade the co-opting of colleagues to fill vacant positions of tribunes. Its purpose was to prevent the patricians from pressuring the tribunes to appoint colleagues sympathetic to or chosen from the aristocracy.

CURIA - (plural **curiae**) Curia has two meanings. It can be a building or meeting place for the Senate to meet in, or it can mean a political division of the people.

CURIA HOSTILIA - Built by King Tullus Hostilius. After the overthrow of the monarchy in 509 BC, the Curia Hostilia became the main meeting place for the Roman Republic Senate, and was perhaps the single most important building in Roman politics. While the Curia Hostilia was the main meeting place for the Senate, it was not the only place the Senate could meet.

CURIO - The curia was presided over by a curio (pl.: curiones), who was always at least 50 years old, and was elected for life. The curio undertook the religious affairs of the curia. He was assisted by another priest, known as the flamen curialis.

CURULE AEDILE - The curule aediles were the magistrates originally chosen from the patricians, however it then changed to alternating years. Responsible for the care and supervision of the markets and they also issued edicts, mainly rules as to buying and selling, and contracts for bargain and sale. They could also act as judges. The privileges of the curule aediles included a fringed toga, a curule chair, and the right to ancestral masks.

CURULE CHAIR – A style of chair reserved in ancient Rome for the use of the highest government dignitaries and usually made like a foldable, backless stool with curved legs. Often inlaid with ivory, with or without arms, it was a sign of power and was bestowed on such officials as the dictator, master of the horse, censor, consul, praetor, interrex, curule aedile, and later, the emperor.

DECEMVIRS – A special commission of ten members who ruled in place of consuls in ancient Rome circa 451-450 BC. Their primary purpose was to draw up Rome's first code of law, The Laws of the Twelve Tables. Because of their abuse of power, it was abandoned after two years.

DICTATOR – The dictator was the highest official in the Roman Republic that was appointed in an emergency. Usually, a dictator was appointed to conduct military campaigns and to quell civil unrest. The dictator was given full power in the pursuit of his cause and his authority was nearly absolute. However, he could only pursue the task for which he was appointed. As soon as the task was completed the dictator must resign.

DUUMVIR – (duumviri plural) A magistracy of two men who were assigned specific jobs. Early on they had charge of the Sibylline Books which they referred to in dangerous times to see what the gods demanded for the sins of the people. Later they could be judges or they could be assigned to administer the sacred rites or deal with public finance or run elections in the comitium.

EQUITES - The *equites* ('horse' or 'cavalrymen', though sometimes referred to as "knights" in English), made up of patricians in the early Roman Republic, constituted the second of the property-based classes of ancient Rome, ranking below the senatorial class. A member of the equestrian order was known as an *eques*.

EXODIA - Humorous verses often performed between serious plays by young patrician males only, who were not looked down on.

FASCES - A bundle of wooden rods with a projecting blade bound together by leather thongs and carried by a *lictor* (bodyguard) in ancient Rome as a symbol of a magistrate's power. Fasces represented that a man held authority.

FASTI – Ancient Roman *fasti* were calendars that recorded religious observances and officially commemorated events. They were usually displayed at a prominent public location such as a major temple.

FETIAL – A type of priest in ancient Rome. They formed a collegium devoted to Jupiter as the patron of good faith. The duties of the fetials included advising the Senate on foreign affairs and international treaties. They were sent to foreign states making formal proclamations of peace or war. They were also used to confirm treaties with foreign states.

FLAMEN - (pl: flamines) A priest assigned to the worship of one deity only. There were 15 *flamines*. The most important were Dialis, Martialis, and Quirinalis, who represented Jupiter, Mars, and Quirinus, respectively. A flamen was picked from the patrician class and led by the *Pontifex Maximus*. They had a distinctive dress, its most notable feature being the *apex*, a conical cap. They held daily sacrifices, and they were subject to strict rules and taboos. Their wives, the *flaminicae*, were their helpers and were also subject to the same rules.

FORMER CONSUL - A prior consul who is called upon for various duties. They tend to be left behind to manage the City.

GABINE CINCTURE - The *cinctus Gabinus* was a way of wearing the toga and thought to have originated in the town of Gabii. It was also later claimed to have been part of the Etruscan priests' clothing. The cincture allowed free use of both arms, particularly when worn during combat and later in some religious rituals, particularly those involving use of the toga to cover the head (capite velato).

GREAT GAMES – There were two kinds of Roman games: sacred or religious games and games of physical prowess. At first the games of the early Roman Republic had religious significance, thanking the gods for help during a battle. Then later the 'secular' games were purely for entertainment, some lasting two weeks.

GUARDIAN – In ancient Rome, all women were under an adult male guardian. That guardian was the oldest male in the household be it a father, grandfather, husband, uncle, or even oldest male child. The wife of the guardian was responsible for taking care of the home and family.

HASTATI - The newer or inexperienced foot soldiers who were the first line of defense armed with spears or javelins.

HISTRIONES - Dancers with mimic gestures to the music of a flute. Introduced by Etruscans who were hired to perform. Later non-citizens, freed-men, strangers or slaves learned the dance to perform. They were looked down upon and not allowed to be citizens or serve as soldiers.

ICILIAN LAW - By the *Icilian Law* the land on the Aventine Hill was deemed to be public land and divided into plots for the plebeians. The patricians were compensated for the value of their buildings already there. It was considered important for the independence of the plebeians that the patricians should not be their landlords, and thus able to control their votes.

IDES - For the months of March, May, July and October, the Ides fell on the 15th day. In every other month, the Ides fell on the 13th day. The third day of the Ides of August refers to August 15th which is the third day of a yearly celebration.

INTERNATIONAL LAW - Jus Gentium - Law of Nations. Early international law was religion-based and was about the concept of the "just war" (*bellum justum*), which could only be declared with a ritual by the fetial priests before any fighting could occur. Foreign ambassadors were protected by the *ius gentium*, and it was not only a religious violation to harm an envoy but the violation of international law.

INTERREGES see **INTERREX**

INTERREX – (pl: **interreges**) Initially, the interrex was appointed after the death of the king of Rome until the election of his successor, hence its name – a ruler "between kings" (Latin *inter reges*). The interrex position was retained during the Roman Republic when both consuls or consular tribunes were unable to assume their duties, usually due to elections being blocked. An interrex ruled for only five days, and sometimes many in a row would be appointed when there was no decision, the record being fifteen interreges in 326 BC. Chosen from among the senators, the position was often used to stop the plebeians from reaching power or passing laws during the Conflict of Orders.

INTERREGNUM – (pl: interregna) A period when normal government is suspended, especially between successive reigns.

JUGERA A jugera was a Roman unit of area, equivalent to a rectangle 240 Roman feet in length and 120 feet in width (0.623 acre). The *jugerum* contained 28,800 square feet, while the English acre contains 43,560.

LECTISTERNIUM - A supplication ceremony, consisting of a meal offered to gods and goddesses spread on couches. The ceremony took place "for the first time" in Rome in the year 399 BC, after a plague had caused the Sibylline Books to be consulted by the duumviri sacris faciundis, the two priestly officials who maintained the archive. Again in 347 BC ten men were sent to check the Sibylline Books during another plague. Three couches were prepared for three pairs of gods – Apollo and Latona – Hercules and Diana – Mercury and Neptune. The feast lasted for eight (or seven) days, and was also celebrated by private individuals. The citizens kept an open house, quarrels were forgotten, debtors and prisoners were released, and everything was done to banish sorrow.

LEX CANULEIA – The Lex Canuleia, established in 445 B.C. in ancient Rome, permitted plebeians to marry patricians, promoting equality between the social classes and advancing towards a more just and fair society. Five years earlier, as part of the process of establishing the Twelve Tables of Roman law, the second decemvirate had placed severe restrictions on the plebeian order, including a prohibition on the intermarriage of patricians and plebeians.

LEX PUBLILIA - This law allowed plebeians to vote for their own plebeian tribunes in their own assembly, held in the Comita Tributa, instead of it being supervised and influenced by patricians.

LEX SACRATA – Not technically a law, this was an oath sworn by the plebeians to protect the plebeian tribunes and to punish with death anyone who should harm the holders of this office. Also, at times of military emergency, the compulsorily drafted soldiers swore to follow their commanders to the death.

LEX TRABONIA - See **TREBONIAN LAW**

LIBRI LINTEI - See **LINEN BOOKS**

LICTOR - A public officer, who were bodyguards for the chief Roman magistrates. A lictor was strong, capable of physical work. They were exempted from military service, received a salary, and were organized in a group. Often, they were personally chosen by the magistrate they were supposed to serve. The lictors had to inflict punishment on those who were condemned by the magistrates. Originally, lictors were chosen from the plebeians, but later they seemed to have been freedmen. They carried wooden rods held together with leather surrounding axes that symbolized the power to carry out capital punishment. They followed the magistrate wherever he went, including the Forum, his house, temples, and the baths.

LINEN BOOKS – The *libri lintei*, also known as the "linen rolls," were a collection of Etruscan books in ancient Rome written on linen, possibly from notes taken on linen clothing. All have been lost except a single Etruscan Liber Linteus, because it had been used as a mummy wrapping. The only way we know of them is from references by Roman authors who refer to them in their writings of history or mythology.

LUSTRUM - The lustrum was originally a sacrifice for making amends and purification offered by one of the censors in the Campus

Martius after the taking of the census was over. The sacrifice was often in the form of an animal sacrifice, known as a suovetaurilia. These censuses were taken at five-year intervals, thus a *lūstrum* came to refer to the five-year inter-census period.

MAGISTER EQUITUM - See **MASTER OF THE HORSE**

MANTLET - In ancient times, the Mantlet was typically constructed of natural materials and wood. It would form a defensive wall or shield that soldiers could use as a cover from arrows.

MASTER OF THE HORSE – The Master of the Horse (Latin: Magister Equitum) in the Roman Republic was a position appointed and dismissed by the Roman dictator, and expired when the dictator resigned, typically a term of six months. He served as the dictator's main lieutenant. In the dictator's absence, the Magister Equitum stepped in as his representative, and exercised the same powers as the dictator. It was usually necessary for the Magister Equitum to have already held the office of praetor. Therefore, the Magister Equitum was entitled to the insignia of a praetor, the toga praetexta and an escort of six lictors.

MILITARY TRIBUNES WITH CONSULAR AUTHORITY – See **CONSULAR TRIBUNES**

MURAL CROWN - A crown which represents city walls, towers, or fortresses awarded to a soldier who first climbed the wall of a besieged city or fortress and successfully places the flag representing his army upon it.

NEW MAN - (Novus homo) The first of his family to attain consul status. The term was used with scorn to belittle the newcomer as the patricians tried to keep themselves exclusive. Becoming a consul automatically made you a senator, however as the new man you were not treated well. This would change in time.

OVATION - A general who did not earn a triumph might be granted an *ovatio*, in which he walked or rode on horseback, wearing the purple-bordered toga of an ordinary magistrate and a wreath of myrtle.

PALISADES - Palisade derives from the Latin word *"palus"*, meaning "stake", specifically when used side by side to create a wooded defensive wall. Roman soldiers usually carried 3 or 4 long stakes which were used in multiple ways.

PLEBEIAN TRIBUNES – These tribunes could advocate and propose legislation on behalf of the plebeians, and veto the actions of the magistrates or other officials. See Tribunes of the People.

POMERIUM - The pomerium was originally an area of ground on both sides of the city walls. Livy states that it was an Etruscan tradition to consecrate this area by augury and that it was technically unlawful to inhabit or to farm the area of the pomerium, which in part had the purpose of preventing buildings from being erected close to the wall.

PONTIFEX MAXIMUS – The Pontifex Maximus was chief high priest of the College of Pontiffs.. He did not serve for a fixed period but for life, and he remained, officially, a citizen. They were responsible for the Roman state religion as a whole and for several religious positions such as the augures, the decemviri sacris faciundis and the fetiales. Because the Pontifex Maximus was not a real magistrate, he was not allowed to wear the toga with the purple border. The Pontifex Maximus was also responsible for the eighteen priestesses of the goddess Vesta (Vestal Virgins).

PONTIFF – The pontiffs, (pontifices), or priests, cared for sacred matters which were ceremonies relating to the worship of the gods, especially sacrifice and prayer and about the proper addressing of people to gods and people to people, when divine matters were also important.

PORTA PRINCIPALIS – One of the main side gates into a legions' camp.

PRAEROGATIVE CENTURIES - The *praerogatives* were the eighteen centuries of knights, which voted first; if they agreed, the other centuries were not called.

PRAETEXTA - A toga with a broad purple border worn by certain magistrates and priests and by young boys until they assumed the toga virilis when reaching manhood.

PRAETOR – Magistrates ranking below consul. A man acting in one of two official capacities: the commander of an army, and as an elected magistrate who had the role of a judge. They often exercised extensive authority in the government in the absence of consuls. A man had to serve as praetor before being elected as a consul.

PRIMUS PILUS - The highest ranking centurion of the first cohort of a Roman legion. He was a career soldier and an experienced advisor to the legate (his boss).

PRINCIPES - The second line of foot soldiers after the *hastati* who were more experienced and fought with sword and shield.

PRO CONSUL - In the ancient Roman Republic, a pro consul was a consul whose powers had been extended for a specific period after his regular term of one year, often as a representative of the current consul and usually as a general in a battle.

PRODIGY - Phenomenon, portent, wonder, prognostication, prophecy. They are signs of nature in the form of lightning, earthquakes, apparitions of light or fire, volcanic eruptions, plagues of locusts, a rain of stones or blood, sweating or bleeding statues of gods, but also monstrosities among humans and animals and more.

PUBLICOLA - See **VALERIUS**

QUAESTOR – An elected official who supervised the state treasury and conducted audits. When assigned to provincial governors, the duties were mainly administrative and logistical, but also could expand to encompass military leadership and command.

RAMPART - The first step in a Roman siege was usually to surround the city by building a wall (rampart) or series of fortifications, cutting off all supplies and reinforcements to the defenders. This allowed the Romans to isolate the city and deprive the defenders of food, water, and other essentials.

ROSTRA – The Rostra was a large platform built in the city of Rome that stood during the republican and imperial periods. Speakers would stand on the rostra and face the north side of the Comitium towards the senate house and deliver orations to those assembled in between.

RUFULI - There are two kinds of military tribunes, the first consisting of those called *Rufuli* which are ordinarily appointed in the army; the second are the *comitiati*, who are designated at the Comitia Centuriata in Rome from which the Consuls and Consular Tribunes, Praetors, etc. are elected.

SACRED LAW - See **LEX SACRATA**

SALII -(Latin: "Dancers") A priesthood usually associated with the worship of Mars, the god of war. The twelve *Salii* were patrician youths who used song and dance as part of religious ritual. They were dressed as warriors with an embroidered tunic, a breastplate, a short red cloak, a sword, and a spiked headdress. They were given twelve bronze shields called *ancilia*, which resembled a figure eight. One of the shields was said to have fallen from heaven in the reign of King Numa and eleven copies were made to protect the identity of the sacred shield. It was prophesied that as long as the shield is safe so would the Roman people be safe. The Salii are sometimes credited with the opening and closing of the war cycle which would last from March to October.

SIBYLLINE BOOKS - The Sibylline Books were a collection of Greek rhymed verses that, according to tradition, were purchased from a sibyl by the last king of Rome, Lucius Tarquinius Superbus, and were consulted in moments of crises through the history of the Roman Republic and the Empire.

SOLON - In 594 BC in Greece, Solon was a ruler who instituted reforms to help Athenian society. Athenian citizens had the right to participate in assembly meetings. He started a wider range of property classes rather than just the aristocracy. His constitutional reforms included establishing four property classes. The classifications were based on how much money a man's estate made per year. This allowed every free citizen of Athens who owned property to have some influence in government. Under these reforms, the boule (a council of 400 members, with 100 citizens from each of Athens' four tribes) ran daily affairs and set the political agenda. Another major contribution to democracy was Solon's setting up an Assembly, which was open to all the male citizens. Solon also made significant economic reforms including canceling existing debts, freeing debtors, and no longer allowing borrowing on the security of one's own person as a means of restructuring enslavement and debt in Athenian society.

SPOLIA OPIMA — The spolia opima were the armor, arms, and other effects that an ancient Roman general stripped from the body of an opposing general he killed in hand-to-hand combat which was then brought back to Rome and dedicated at the temple of Jupiter Feretrius on the Capitoline Hill. Aulus Cornelius Cossus was a Roman general in the early Republic who is famous for being the second (secunda) Roman, after Romulus (prima), to be awarded the spolia opima, Rome's highest military honor.

SURETY - (Sureties, plural) - Essentially a bond. A surety is an entity or an individual who assumes the duty of paying the debt in the event that a debtor fails or is not able to make the payments. The bronze nuggets, **a**es rude, usually weighed 5 pounds each. In the case of Caeso, each surety at 3,000 aes rude would be 15,000 pounds. Ten sureties would be 150,000 pounds.

SUTLER - A person who followed an army and sold provisions to the soldiers. The traditional sutler followed troops and sold them supplies at hugely inflated prices.

TERENTILLIAN LAW - Proposed by Caius Terentillius Arsa in 462 BC that five men be chosen to write down the laws establishing consular power. The senate disagreed. After much squabbling over many years three men were sent to Athens to learn the laws and customs and to return with information. By 448 BC the Law of Twelve Tables was established by the ten decemvirs who were charged with creating it.

TESTUDO - (plural Testudines) The testudo or tortoise formation was a type of shield-wall formation commonly used by the Roman legions during battles, particularly sieges. Used for protection against attacks from above, consisting either of a movable arched structure or of overlapping shields held by the soldiers over their heads.

TOGA PRAETEXTA – Adopted by the Romans from the Etruscans. It was a white toga with a broad purple stripe on its border, worn over a tunic with two broad, vertical purple stripes. It was a formal costume for curule magistrates in their official functions, and traditionally, the Kings of Rome.

TORQUE - A necklace ring worn by both men and women. It was made of rigid metal and often the metal was twisted. It usually had an ornamental opening in the front.

TREBONIAN LAW - The Lex Trebonia was a law passed in 448 BC to forbid the plebeian tribunes from co-opting colleagues to fill vacant positions. Its purpose was to prevent the patricians from pressuring the plebeian tribunes to appoint colleagues sympathetic to or chosen from the patricians.

TRIARII – The triarii were the oldest and wealthiest soldiers, usually in their thirties, and in battle they stood as the third line of defense behind the younger hastati soldiers and the more experienced principes.

TRIBUNE OF THE PLEBEIANS – (aka plebeian tribunes) A plebeian tribune was a protector of the common people or plebeians. He had the power to veto legislation in the Senate and could introduce legislation as well. He could protect a plebeian from unjust punishment by a magistrate and prosecute and administer sentences.

TRIUMPH - A procession that was the highest honor bestowed upon a victorious general in the ancient Roman Republic; it was the summit of a Roman aristocrat's career. Triumphs were granted and paid for by the Senate and held in the city of Rome; although sometimes the victorious general would pay for his own. To triumph in Roman republican times a man was required to have been a general having complete command of the army and cavalry who had won a battle in the region he was assigned to, killing at least 5,000 of the enemy and ending the war. In the procession the general wore a toga with a purple stripe and rode in a chariot. The triumph began with a procession from the Triumphal Gate in the Campus Martius to the Temple of Jupiter on the Capitoline Hill, passing through the Forum and the Via Sacra along streets adorned with flowers and lined with people shouting, "Io triumphe!"

A general who did not earn a triumph might be granted an *ovation*, in which he walked or rode on horseback, wearing the purple-bordered toga of an ordinary magistrate and a wreath of myrtle.

VALERIUS - Publius Valerius Publicola (or Poplicola) came from the wealthy Valerii family of Sabine origin. He was one of four Roman patricians who were the leaders to overthrow the monarchy. He became a Roman consul along with his colleague Lucius Junius Brutus in 509 BC, which was considered to be the first year of the Roman Republic. His father was Volesus Valerius, and his brothers were Marcus Valerius Volesus and Manius Valerius Volesus Maximus. He had a daughter, Valeria, and possibly a son or grandson who was also named Publius Valerius Publicola who served as consul in 475 BC and 460 BC.

VESTAL VIRGINS - Vestal Virgins were young girls chosen between the ages of 6 and 10 by the Pontifex Maximus. They remained as virgins for 30 years. Afterward they could marry, but most chose to remain free. To be chosen as a Vestal Virgins you had to be of the required age, be freeborn and have respectable parents who were both alive, and have no physical or mental problems. Living in the House of the Vestal Virgins on the Roman Forum, near the Temple of Vesta, their duties included tending the perpetual fire in the Temple of Vesta, keeping their vow of chastity, fetching water from a sacred spring (they could not drink from the city water-supply system), preparing ritual food, caring for objects in the temple's inner sanctuary, and officiating at the Vestalia (June 7–15), the period of public worship of Vesta. Beatings were rendered for failure to attend to their duties. Breaking the vow of chastity was punished by being buried alive (the blood of a Vestal Virgin could not be spilled). The Vestal Virgins enjoyed privileges not open to married or single women of the same social status, which included freedom from their father's rule and the freedom to handle their own property.

VINEAE - The Romans preferred to assault enemy walls by building earthen ramps (*agger*) or simply scaling the walls with ladders. Soldiers working at the ramps were protected by shelters called *vineae*, that were arranged to form a long corridor. Convex wicker shields were used to form a screen to protect the front of the corridor during construction of the ramp.Soldiers were able to lift them and move them together in a row towards the enemy wall. They were covered with panels of woven twigs to give protection from archers. The roofs may have been reinforced with a double layer of timber boards to protect against large stones being hurled at them from above. The entire exterior would be covered with wetted animal skins to protect against the arrows. The Romans were able to create protected galleries by joining several of these together. This enabled them to get close to outer walls and undermine them or build ramps up to them.

Made in United States
Orlando, FL
27 December 2024

56542061R00086